COLONEL JOHN PICKERING'S REGIMENT OF FOOT 1644 - 1645

Glenn Foard

WHITSTABLE AND WALSALL

Cover illustration:
Pickering's regiment depicted on
Streeter's engraving of the Battle of Naseby
(Northamptonshire Libraries and Information Service)

PRYOR PUBLICATIONS

75 Dargate Road, Yorkletts,
Whitstable, Kent CT5 3PE
Tel. & Fax : (0227) 274655

Specialist in Facsimile Reproductions

MEMBER OF
INDEPENDENT PUBLISHERS GUILD

ISBN 0 946014 25 6

A CIP Record for this book is available from the British Library

£1 from the sale of each copy of this book will be donated to
the Titchmarsh Church restoration fund

Printed and bound by
Whitstable Litho Printers Ltd., Whitstable, Kent

THIS BOOK IS DEDICATED TO
ALL THE PAST, PRESENT AND FUTURE
MEMBERS OF
COLONEL JOHN PICKERING'S REGIMENT OF FOOT

Acknowledgements

I would like to thank all those who have given advice and help in the preparation of this book. In particular Mrs Griffiths, Assistant Librarian at St.Catherine's College, for providing detailed information from the college archives. Also Barry Denton, who read and commented on an early draft of the book, the staff of the Public Record Office and of the Northamptonshire Record Office, A.Turton of Basing House, D.H.Ford of Oundle School, T.Thom of Gray's Inn and L.J.Bradshaw of the National Portrait Gallery.

Figures 11, 29 and 31 are reproduced with the permission of the Controller of Her Majesty's Stationery Office. Northamptonshire Record Society have given permission to reproduce figures 12 and 24. All other engravings and photographs, unless otherwise stated, are from the author's collection.

I must make special mention of Roger Benton who founded Colonel John Pickering's Regiment of Foot within the Sealed Knot in 1988. If the regiment had not been created within that re-enactment society then this book would never have been written. I must also acknowledge Andy Chandler, who originally had the idea of writing a history of the regiment. It had been intended that we write the book together, before his departure to Hungary. Alan Pryor, a fellow member of Pickering's Regiment in the Sealed Knot, has made publication possible. Last but not least I must thank my wife Anne. She has drawn all the maps and visited most of the sites with me. Without Anne's encouragement and understanding the book would never have been finished.

Abbreviations

BL	British Library.
DNB	Dictionary of National Biography.
HMC	Historic Manuscripts Commission.
NRO	Northamptonshire Record Office.
PRO	Public Record Office.
RCHM	Royal Commission on Historical Monuments
Sprigge	J.Sprigge, 1647, *'Anglia Rediviva'*.
T.T.	Thomason Tracts, British Library.
VCH	Victoria County History.

Contents

List of Illustrations

Figures

Tables

Preface

This short history traces the life of John Pickering and takes the story of his regiment from its creation in March 1644 up to the time of Pickering's death in November 1645. A brief postscript then considers the later history of the regiment under the command of John Hewson.

The idea of writing such a history came soon after we joined the newly formed Pickering's Regiment in the Sealed Knot in 1988. None of us knew very much about the history of the regiment and that needed to be redressed. I also found it a particularly interesting subject because John Pickering was, like myself, a Northamptonshire man.

The task has taken far longer to complete than was ever intended. This is partly because other research and writing took precedence, but also because, to my surprise, there was a large body of material to work through. Indeed, the regiment's involvement in many of the key events of the Civil War opened too many avenues of research! To ensure publication in time for the 350th anniversary of the formation of the regiment, I reluctantly decided to leave some potential sources for others to explore at a later date. I hope however that enough evidence has been brought together to hold the interest of the reader and to show the important role that Colonel John Pickering's Regiment of Foot played in the English Civil War.

Glenn Foard
Earls Barton
January 1994

Introduction

Most historians trace the lineage of the British Army from the regiments created at the restoration of Charles II. However, it was during the turmoil of the Civil Wars and Interregnum, in the middle decades of the 17th century, that England's first truly professional army was established.

The origins of this professionalism must be sought in East Anglia, the secure base of parliamentarian power throughout the war. It was here, under the influence Oliver Cromwell, that the Eastern Association army was developed, by 1644, into the best organised of Parliament's forces. With the lessons learnt in the Eastern Association, it was Cromwell again who was instrumental in the formation, in 1645, of the New Model Army, which came to eclipse all other military forces. At first it was very different from later English armies. The lessons of how to organise and maintain an effective standing army were only just being learnt.

Colonel John Pickering's Regiment of Foot was created in these formative years. The two years of his command were a crucial period in the establishment of England's first standing army. Pickering and his regiment were near the heart of that process.

Unlike later regiments, with their formal identities, these Civil War regiments were known by the name of their commander. Indeed, much of their character seems to have derived from the character of their Colonel. These commanders were the men that led a revolution, and the nature of that revolution was determined by their beliefs and attitudes. It is therefore appropriate that we start by looking at the character and background of John Pickering himself.

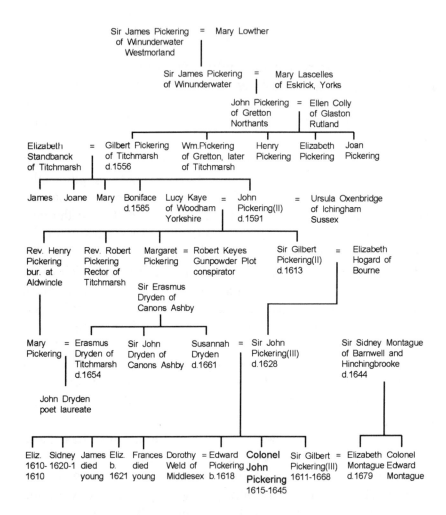

Figure 1 : A simplified family tree of the Pickerings.

Chapter 1

The Pickering Family

The Pickerings originated from Westmorland, descended from Sir James Pickering of 'Winunderwater'.[1] By the early 16th century they had moved to Gretton in Northamptonshire. Both of the sons of John Pickering of Gretton moved to Titchmarsh, in the same county. By 1525 John's second son, Gilbert, was the fourth wealthiest householder in the village[2]. So began the alternating sequence of Gilbert and John Pickering of Titchmarsh, which continued down to the 18th century. Gilbert(I) became the lord of the manor, by purchase, in 1553. This was a substantial estate comprising 160 houses and 100 cottages, a watermill and 3000 acres of land.

By the late 16th century the Pickerings had risen to local prominence in the eastern part of Northamptonshire, one of the new class of landed gentry that developed during the Tudor period. Befitting their new status, the family came to play a role in local administration and in the running of the local militia. This foreshadowed the role they would play during the Civil War. In a 'View of Arms' taken in 1586, during the war with Spain, the three *"gentry suitable for leader"* in the eastern division of the county were William Brown of Oundle, Edward Montague, and Gilbert Pickering(II). However Gilbert did not, apparently, take up a commission as captain of a militia company.[3] Gilbert was succeeded by his son, John. Sir John Pickering(III) married Susannah the daughter of Sir Erasmus Dryden of Canons Ashby, in western Northamptonshire. Sir John and Susannah were the parents of Colonel John Pickering.

1

During the Civil War the driving force behind the parliamentarian cause in Northamptonshire, as in other counties, was a core of a few families of gentry. Many of these families were closely linked not only in their political and religious views but also related in marriage.[4] Already by 1626 the Pickerings and the Drydens were joined in opposition to the king. Sir John Pickering(III) and Sir Erasmus Dryden were imprisoned, together with John Hampden, for refusing to pay forced loans to Charles I. The Montagues were another family linked to the Pickerings by marriage who were to play an important role both nationally and locally during the Civil War and Commonwealth. These three families were represented on the Committee for Association for Northampton in 1643-4 by Edward Montague, Sir John Dryden, and Sir Gilbert Pickering.

Three of Sir John Pickering's children reached adulthood. All the other sisters and brothers died young. As eldest son, Gilbert(III), born in 1611, became lord of the manor when Sir John died. Charles I made Gilbert a baronet in 1626. After studying at Cambridge, he trained as a lawyer at Gray's Inn, London. In 1638 he married Elizabeth, daughter of Sir Sidney Montague of Hinchingbrook, Huntingdonshire. Elizabeth is the only member of this generation of the Pickering family for which a portrait has been traced.[5] Gilbert was elected an MP for Northamptonshire to the Short Parliament of 1640 and, later in that year, for the Long Parliament. He became Deputy Lieutenant of the county and a member of the County Committee during the Civil War. Gilbert raised money for Parliament and served on Committees for the sequestration of delinquents and for settling the militia. He also raised, though did not command, a dragoon regiment in eastern Northamptonshire. In 1649 Gilbert was appointed as a commissioner and judge in the trial of Charles I, though wisely he attended only two sittings and did not sign the death warrant. During the Commonwealth he rose to a position of

2

considerable national influence, as a member of the Council of State and as Commissioner in various posts. Finally in 1655 he was appointed Lord Chamberlain to the Lord Protector. He was described disparagingly after the Restoration as a Committee man and sequestrator.[6] It was due only to the intervention of his brother-in-law, Edward Montague, Earl of Sandwich, that Gilbert obtained a pardon from Charles II.[7]

The youngest son, Edward Pickering, was born in 1618. He was also educated as a lawyer, at Lincoln's Inn, but played no significant role during the war. 'Ned', as he was affectionately known to his friends, was a companion of Samuel Pepys and is frequently described in Pepys' diary. Apparently he did not, at least after the Restoration, practice the same religious abstinence as had his brothers. In political views he was also apparently less firm than his brothers for Edward, probably influenced by Edward Montague, travelled to the continent in 1660 to swear allegiance to Charles II before the Restoration.

The Pickerings had long been known for their strong puritan beliefs. In this they reflected the strength of puritanism in eastern Northamptonshire, which had developed rapidly and become strongly entrenched in the Peterborough diocese during the second half of the 16th century.[8] Robert Browne, whose 'Brownism' developed into the Independent form of puritanism, that in its turn led to Congregationalism, was vicar of the parish of Thorpe Achurch from 1591 to 1630.[9] The parish was just three miles to the north of Titchmarsh. The Pickerings were therefore close to the very heart of the religious sect, the Independents, which was, through the Civil War, to gain control of first the army and then the country. Gilbert Pickering was described after the Restoration as "*first a presbyterian, then an Independent, then a Brownist and afterwards an Anabaptist. He was a most furious, fiery implacable man, and was the principal agent in casting out most of the learned clergy.*"[10] Even after the Restoration, as late

3

Figure 2 : The parish church at Titchmarsh lay close by the Pickerings' manor house. The chamber over the porch was a private pew of the Pickering family. The chimney which served the fireplace in the chamber can be seen at the far side of the porch.

as the 1670s, Lady Pickering was still holding Congregationalist meetings in the manor house at Titchmarsh.

It is of course true that, as in any family, not every member shared the same beliefs. So we find, in the early 17th century, that one of the Gunpowder Plot conspirators, Robert Keyes, had married into the family. Similarly, John Dryden, cousin to John, Gilbert and Edward Pickering, who had served as secretary to Gilbert while he was Lord Chamberlain, developed extreme royalist views after the Restoration.

Titchmarsh, the Pickerings' family home for more than two centuries, is today a small, pleasant, stone built village typical of Northamptonshire's Nene valley. It retains many of its 17th century buildings and, despite the many changes that have occurred over the last 350 years, one can still gain a feeling for the character of the village within which John Pickering grew up. The original fortified manor house in Titchmarsh had already gone by the 17th century. It now survives as just an earthwork of a moated enclosure and it lies immediately north of the field called Little Park on the 1779 map (figure 3). This Medieval manor was demolished in about 1558 when John Pickering(II) removed his residence to a new site. He built a new manor house on the south side of the church and it was here that our John Pickering was born and brought up. The building was described in the early 18th century as "*embattled on the south side*" and having "*an embattled turret.*"[11]

The development of the gardens and parkland around the manor house had occurred at the expense of the church. It is recorded that by the mid 17th century Sir Gilbert Pickering having "*taken in part of the Churchyard into his gardens, hath brought his wall so nigh to the Porch, that he hath built a closet over it...*"[12] This room over the porch was blocked up after the Pickerings ceased to live in the village, but the view from it into the church was reopened and a new window inserted, earlier this century.

Unfortunately today the room over the porch is no longer floored, the external staircase has gone and the fireplace has been removed. However, the elaborate chimney built by the Pickering's, for the fires which provided comfort on cold winter Sundays, is still there. This private pew over the porch is a good example of the social attitudes of the family, as is the lace and finery of the clothes seen in the portrait of Lady Elizabeth, Gilbert's wife. They may have had extreme puritan beliefs, but this did not extend to the social levelling promoted by men such as John Lilburne. The Pickerings were in much the same mould as their associates the Cromwells.

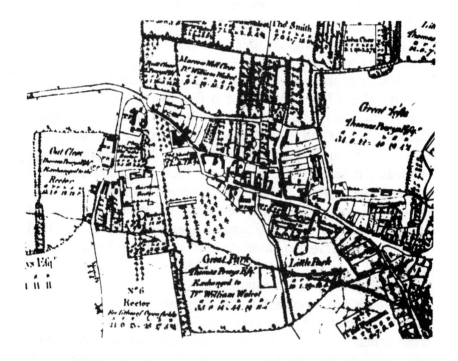

Figure 3 : Titchmarsh village in 1779. The Pickerings' manor house lay immediately to the south of the church, in the north western corner of Great Park. (Northamptonshire Record Office)

They would challenge the religious and political order but with regard to the social order they were staunchly conservative.

The manor house is said to have been to the south of the church. If this is correct then it had already been demolished when the Inclosure map of the village was drawn in 1779. There are a few slight earthworks just outside the churchyard gate, in the area called the Old Yard on the 1779 map, which might be part of the manor house. However, most of the site lay further south and is now levelled or built over.[13] Because the Pickering manor house is long since gone, to gain a feeling for the home environment within which John grew up one must visit his grandparents' home, Canons Ashby House, in western Northamptonshire. It is now owned by the National Trust and retains much of the character it must have had in the early 17th century. To judge from the Hearth Tax assessment of 1662, the Pickering manor house was an even more substantial residence than that at Canons Ashby, with 23 hearths compared to 18.[14] The Pickering children were probably frequent visitors to the Drydens' country house and would have been familiar with the 16th century tower, Great Hall and the 'Great Chamber' with its impressive plaster ceiling.

The Pickering family continued to live in and to dominate the village of Titchmarsh into the 18th century. The family title eventually became extinct in 1749.[15] There are several monuments to the Pickerings in the parish church, in the family's burial place at the east end of the north aisle. All date to the late 17th and 18th century. Some were painted by Elizabeth Creed, daughter of Gilbert Pickering(III), a very talented amateur painter. The most important monument is the large chest tomb, over the family vault, with a monumental inscription above. The latter details many of the family buried in the vault. They include Edward Pickering, Sir Gilbert Pickering(III), and their father, Sir John Pickering(III). Though mentioned on the tomb, Colonel John Pickering was not buried there.

The tomb carries the family coat of arms. By the late 17th century however it was quartered with that of the Lasselle family and the arms of two other families to which the Pickerings had been linked in marriage. At the time of the Civil War the coat of arms was far simpler, the Pickering lion being quartered only with the arms of the Lasselles. In such a strongly religious family as the Pickerings it is appropriate that ermine, the colour of the field of their arms, should signify religion or holiness.

Figure 4 : The Pickering coat of arms as it was in the mid 17th century.

8

The arms are emblazoned thus: **'on a shield four quarterly ermine lion rampant azure crowned armed and langued or argent three chaplets gules on a wreath of argent and gules a lions jamb erect and erased azure armed or'.** That is, a quartered shield the 1st and 4th quarters containing the Pickerings' blue lion rampant with gold crown, claws and tongue placed on an ermine ground. In the 2nd and 3rd quarters are three red chaplets or wreaths, two at the top and one underneath on a silver ground. The crest, resting on a wreath of silver and red, is a blue lion's limb torn from the body, upright with gold claws.[16]

It was into this puritan family of Northamptonshire gentry that John Pickering was born in 1615. The second son to John Pickering(III), he was baptised at Titchmarsh on the 3rd of December.[17] Although his grandfather had died in 1613, his grandmother, Elizabeth, survived until 1620, when John Pickering was five years old. Undoubtedly she would have been a familiar figure in his early life. It seems likely that John will also have been a frequent visitor to his mother's home at Canons Ashby, the Dryden family seat. Like the Pickerings, the Drydens had established their estates and influence in the county during the second half of the 16th century. They too were dedicated puritans of long standing. Close by the House they had a private chapel, which still stands today, where from 1608 to 1631 the celebrated and austere puritan preacher John Dod served as family chaplain.

John Pickering's whole environment was therefore one of privilege and influence, yet of strict and extreme religious beliefs. John Milton's description of the typical Independents fits John Pickering very well: "*men of better conditions of life, of families not disgraced if not enobled, of fortunes either ample or moderate.....prepared, not only to debate, but to fight; not only to argue in the senate, but to engage the enemy in the field.*"[18] The course of his adult life, in the context of civil strife, was therefore almost inevitable.

John's education reinforced the effect of his family background. He was educated first at the Laxton School in nearby Oundle, where he was admitted on the 12th January 1627. By this time John was 11 years old. His brother, Edward, who was just 8 years old was also admitted to the school on the same day. Another John Pickering, son of Boniface Pickering of Oundle and a distant relation to John, also attended the school from 1628.[19]

Figure 5 : Laxton School, Oundle, circa 1820. The schoolroom lay on the first floor, overlooking the churchyard. The children are playing amongst the gravestones just as they must have done in John's day. (Northamptonshire Libraries and Information Service)

This free grammar school, which stood next to the churchyard, had been established in 1556 out of the former Guildhall. By the early 17th century it had changed little from the original school which was described in 1565 as "*a very fair hall builded with freestone.*"[20] The schoolroom lay on the first floor of the building, where there were also smaller rooms for the Master and the Usher. During the 17th century the ground floor continued to serve as an almshouse.

From the schoolroom windows John would have looked out over the graveyard to the impressive Medieval church where, as at the school, there was a strong puritan tradition during the early 17th century. Just outside the school door however he would have walked out, at least on a Saturday, into the bustle of the traders and customers on the Cornhill and in the adjacent market square. In the 17th century Oundle was a small, wealthy market town. Today, thanks perhaps in part to the influence of Oundle School, the town retains something of the character it had in John's time. The engraving of the school made in the early 19th century shows children playing in the churchyard in front of the Tudor building, very much as John and his school-friends must have done in the 1620s. The Laxton School was completely rebuilt in 1852 but the new building, which occupies the same site, was constructed very much in the style of the original and so the scene today is probably very similar to that which existed in 1626. However, all that remains of the actual fabric of the original school is the black inscribed stone of 1593, now set above the entrance on the east end of the building. Also surviving is the wooden Master's Chair, made in 1576, which is still in use for special occasions.[21]

The fortunes of the school had reached a low ebb in the years before John attended. However, with the election of Samuel Cob as Master in June 1625, and the appointment of William Dugard as Usher in 1626, the school flourished. It has been said that "*for about a quarter of a century, from the accession of*

11

Charles I until the Civil War, Oundle clearly enjoyed a higher reputation than any other comparable school." In 1626, the year when John was admitted, there were sixty-eight pupils, representing a broad cross section of English society. Though some of the boys were local, others came from elsewhere in the county and some from further afield. They boarded in private houses in the town, and a few with the Master and the Usher in the School House in Church Lane. Boniface Pickering, a distant relation of John's, lived in Oundle at this time and it is possible that John and Edward boarded with them. However, like other boys from the Oundle area, the two brothers probably rode the six miles into town from Titchmarsh every day, except Sundays. Unlike our modern schools, in the 17th century the pupils attended six days a week. At Oundle they also had only about twenty days holiday a year, all apparently taken in December.

Cob proved himself an energetic and effective Master while Dugard is considered to have been a *"brilliant young Usher"*. Dugard later became Master of the Merchant Taylor's School, a noted puritan writer and publisher, and a friend of the Independent puritan poet John Milton. Both Cob and, perhaps most of all, Dugard must have had a significant influence on the young John Pickering, reinforcing the religious ideas that had been instilled by his family. Though both were good teachers they would still, as in any good school of the period, have enforced strict discipline and made regular use of the cane.[22]

After less than five years at Oundle, John progressed to St.Catherine's College, Cambridge, where he was probably admitted in 1629 or 1630.[23] He matriculated as a Fellow Commoner of the College in 1631.[24] Various members of the Pickering family had attended the university at Cambridge, though the particular college varied.[25] Knowing the beliefs of the Pickerings, it seems clear that the choice of St.Catherine's was made on religious grounds. Since Richard Sibbs had been elected

12

Master of St.Catherine's, the College had become a puritan institution. It has been said that this was perhaps the most brilliant period of the College's history. The Fellows included John Arrowsmith, a staunch puritan, William Strong, an Independent and Thomas Goodwin, who in 1649 became chaplain to the Council of State and a favourite of Cromwell. Probably most notable of the tutors there at this time was John Knowles. Knowles was "*a divine who became famous for his extreme puritanism. He emigrated to the New England settlements, but even there he incurred censure for his refusal to use a prayer book and to wear a surplice. But when he returned to England....in 1651 it was reckoned that no less than forty-seven of his former pupils were either Members of Parliament or of the Assembly of Divines.*"[26]

St.Catherine's at this time probably had less than 100 members. The annual intake was about 25, of which only a handful would be Fellow Commoners like John. At their admission they made a five-shilling admission payment and a £2 payment for the purchase of books. Following their matriculation they were expected to make a gift of silver plate. These gifts were engraved with the College's and the Fellow Commoner's coats of arms. The '*pot*' which John had presented was still listed in the College records in 1637. However, following common practice at the time, it was exchanged by the College, along with various other plate, for two silver flagons in January 1638.[27]

Fellow Commoners were privileged undergraduates, and distinguished from them by their gowns. They normally took about a year to matriculate and then spent just one more year at St.Catherine's, before proceeding to an Inn of Court. John however did not transfer for another three years. Perhaps he remained at St.Catherine's working for a degree, as had his brother, but there is no record of the award of a B.A. to John.[28]

Little survives of St.Catherine's College from John Pickering's day, except the buildings of the Walnut Tree Court, at the north western corner of the college, adjacent to Queen's Lane. The rest of the buildings, which fronted the lane, were extensively rebuilt in the late 17th century.[29] At this time St.Catherine's was overshadowed by the larger Queen's College with its more impressive buildings. The great gatehouse which faced St.Catherine's across Queen's Lane still stands today.

John's intense puritan views are clearly seen from his obituary which says *"instead of Drinking, Swearing, Roaring, Carding, Dicing and Drabbing, he spent that little time he had to spare, in the study of the scriptures..."*[30] There seems little doubt that the extreme nature of his puritanism, which later drew violent criticism from presbyterians in the army, owed something to his time at Cambridge. The influence of Knowles and the other puritan Fellows undoubtedly reinforced the already strong beliefs originating from John's family and school background. Was the lay preaching which John practiced, and which caused so much trouble in April 1645, something that he owed to Knowles?

Many students during the 17th century transferred from university to the Inns of Court. So it was that John followed his brother Gilbert to Gray's Inn, London, on the 10th October 1634.[31] The association of the Pickerings with the law, and especially with Gray's Inn, was a long standing one. As early as 1592 the notable puritan, Lewis Pickering had entered Gray's Inn. This Inn of Court was the most popular with families from the Midlands and East Anglia. There is no reason to believe that Gray's Inn fostered a political bias. However, it would have provided John with an environment compatible with his political views, for it tended to produce parliamentarian rather than royalist supporters. Of those that attended the Inn who went on, like John's brother, to become MPs, twice as many supported parliament as supported the king.[32]

Many young men with landed estates simply wanted a legal qualification from the Inns of Court in order to be prepared to act

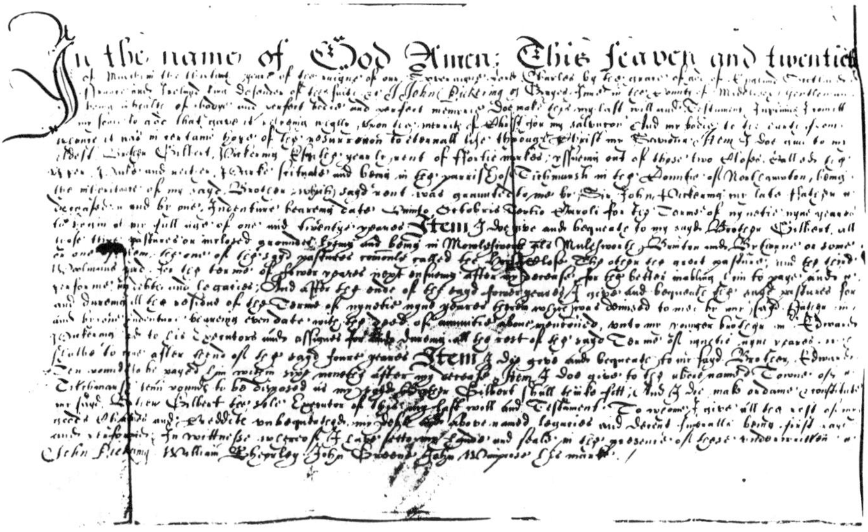
In the name of God Amen: This seaven and twentie

Figure 6 : A copy of John Pickering's will, signed at Gray's Inn, London in 1638.

as magistrates or in political life, rather than as practicing lawyers. John Pickering however, as second son, was left very little land by his father. His will shows he owned just a few closes in Titchmarsh and in the adjacent villages of Molesworth and Bythorn. He therefore had no alternative but to seek a profession.[33]

John was still resident at Gray's Inn in 1638.[34] There is little evidence as to John's activities while there and unfortunately almost the whole of Gray's Inn has been rebuilt since Pickering's time. The Hall, which was constructed in the 16th century, is the only building which survives today with which John would have been familiar.[35]

By November or December 1641, during the dispute with the Scots, he had taken up work for Parliament. He was engaged in diplomatic work, carrying messages to its committee in Scotland. As Sprigge recorded, after Pickering's death, "*he had done the kingdome great service, by riding between England and Scotland before these troubles.*"[36] In May 1642, as events progressed inexorably towards civil war, he was again working for the Lords. He was dispatched to apprehend the keeper of the royal seal, who had secretly escaped from London taking the seal to the king.[37] Once the war began, John was drawn ever more closely to the military action. In October he was sent by the Deputy Lieutenant of Cambridgeshire for fourteen days to collect information on the advance of the enemy.[38] Between November 1642 and February 1643 John was again working as an agent for Parliament. In December and January he was in Scotland, passing on accounts to parliament about the events in the Scottish Privy Council. This was during the early stages of the political manoeuvring which finally led to the entry of the Scottish forces into the war on the side of Parliament.[39]

These letters are the only writing we have by John, and of course they give no insight into his character. The verses of poetry written in 1637, previously attributed to John, are now thought to be by John Pickering, physician, of Aldwincle, Northants.[40]

Chapter 2

The Eastern Association

The Eastern Association had been formed under a parliamentary ordinance of December 1642. This ordinance created a number of regional associations of counties, to achieve a pooling of military resources and hence a more effective war effort. These associations were generally ineffective, but the Eastern Association more than fulfilled its objectives. The Association was first placed under the command of Lord Grey of Warke. He was relieved of command in mid July 1643, for failing to prosecute the war with sufficient vigour, and was replaced in mid August by Edward Montague, Earl of Manchester. This was a time of major setbacks for the parliamentarian cause, with the defeat of Essex's army and the loss of Bristol. The strengthening and reorganisation of the Eastern Association was desperately needed.

As we have seen, in autumn 1642 John Pickering was already working on military matters in Cambridgeshire. He was undoubtedly well known to the Earl of Manchester through Gilbert Pickering's marriage into the Montague family. Gilbert Pickering will also have dealt with the Earl in 1642, when he assisted in arranging the defence of Northampton, as both were members of the Northampton Committee.[41] Like John, the Earl of Manchester had been educated at Cambridge and he may even have been instrumental in gaining Pickering employment in the service of Parliament. It is not surprising therefore to find John being appointed, in August 1643, as Commissary General of the Musters for the Association.[42] The Muster Master received orders, made a general muster of the whole army before it marched, kept a list of

17

Figure 7 : Edward Montague, Earl of Manchester, Major General of the Eastern Association. (Pryor Publications)

the number of arms and the strength of the army, making reviews when required, keeping a record of alterations between every muster and recording those killed, sick, run away or discharged.[43] In this post Pickering was involved in the setting up of the twenty Eastern Association regiments required under the parliamentary ordinance of the 16th August 1643.[44] For example, in late August he was engaged in dealings with Sir Thomas Barrington and the other Deputy Lieutenants of Essex in the mustering of a regiment from that county.[45] His work as Commissary for the Association continued throughout 1643,[46] and apparently up to the 20th of April 1644.[47]

On the 13th of August 1643 the important East Anglian port of King's Lynn declared against Parliament, in anticipation of an advance of the Earl of Newcastle's royalist army into Norfolk.[48] The newly raised Association forces were rushed north to besiege the town. After some weeks Manchester offered the town the opportunity to surrender, before the final assault was launched. John Pickering was one of eight commissioners who met with their royalist counterparts, at Gaywood, several miles to the east of Lynn, to negotiate the treaty of surrender. The debate lasted 24 hours, but was successfully concluded and the surrender took place on the 15th of September 1643.[49] In such situations John's legal training must have proven a great benefit. He was to participate in various similar negotiations over the next two years. During the autumn of 1643 Manchester's army went on to defeat the royalist forces, which were advancing from the north, at Winceby in Lincolnshire. As a General Officer of the Eastern Association army it is likely that, at least for some of the time, John accompanied the army during the autumn campaign. In September he was still referred to as plain "*Mr.John Pickering*".[50] However, at some time following the siege of King's Lynn, late in 1643 or early 1644, he received a commission as Colonel of a regiment of dragoons.[51] By January 1644 he is recorded as Colonel Pickering,

19

when he and Colonel Boynton carried a message for the Earl of Manchester to the House of Lords.[52] That John's commission was this late is confirmed by the fact that later during the war Colonel Montague, whose commission was dated 20th August 1643, had seniority over John.

Pickering's dragoons were an Eastern Association regiment, perhaps from Essex where most of the Association's dragoons were raised.[53] This transfer to the command of a regiment may have been through Oliver Cromwell's influence. His strategy for the development of the Association army was to recruit dedicated men with strong puritan beliefs who were committed to the success of the parliamentarian cause. Cromwell was already moving towards conflict with the Earl of Manchester, over military as well as religious matters. It was perhaps by the commissioning of men like Pickering that he hoped to strengthen his position.

Pickering saw his first military action as a commander in March 1644, at the storming of Hillesden House. Hillesden was the residence of Sir Alexander Denton, who had fortified it as a royalist garrison. The attack was part of a parliamentarian strategy to secure communications north from London and west to Gloucester. This was in the face of royalist advances that had begun in October 1643 with the fortifying of Newport Pagnell. They posed a threat to both London and the Association. It was apparently in response to this that new Association regiments, including Pickering's dragoons, were being raised in late December. The London Trained Bands, under Major General Skippon, were sent to retrieve the situation. Supported by local forces they recovered Newport. They were then joined at Christmas by a small number of Association troops in the storming of the new royalist garrison at Grafton Regis, Northamptonshire. Soon after Grafton fell, the nearby royalist garrison at Towcester was also abandoned. Parliamentarian control of the area was then devolved upon local forces supported by the Eastern Association.[54]

Figure 8 : Hillesden church, Buckinghamshire. Both the church and the manor house, which lay immediately to the east, were fortified in 1644 as a royalist garrison. The holes in the church door are said to have been made by musket balls fired during the siege.

It was at this time that the retreating royalists garrisoned Hillesden House. Colonel Smith defended it with a trench about half a mile long, encircling both house and church. This became the target for the next parliamentarian action. An abortive attack on Hillesden was undertaken by troops from the newly established Newport Pagnell garrison on the 27th of February 1643. To take the house Sir Samuel Luke, governor of Newport, now requested help from the Eastern Association and other local forces.

21

With one thousand local labourers the royalists began digging further trenches around the site and prepared artillery positions for five small pieces received from Oxford. The ditches had not been completed and were in places no more than knee deep when the second parliamentarian attack was launched.[55]

The whole force was under the command of Lieutenant General Cromwell. It included some of Cromwell's horse and some of the Eastern Association foot under Crawford, who were at that time involved in taking ammunition to Gloucester.[56] Amongst the Association infantry, were Colonel Edward Montague's and Colonel Thomas Ayloffe's regiments. Further support came from the major garrisons of Northampton and Newport Pagnell.[57] According to Sir Alexander Denton the parliamentarians had some four thousand horse and foot. On the preceding night Cromwell had been quartered at Steeple Claydon, just over a mile to the southeast of Hillesden and the attack was launched on Sunday 3rd.[58] In the engagement John Pickering *"received a little wound, the first and the last to his death."*[59]

Interestingly one of the royalist reports identifies Pickering by name, suggesting he was already a notable figure: *"Cromwell, Pickering and some others, with eighteen hundred rebels came to Hillesden, girt the house round and stormed it in several places at once, whereby they broke in, the garrison not being sufficient to man the works, nor the works themselves finished."*[60] Once the defences had been overrun, the defenders retreated to the House and Church. In a second assault the parliamentarians took the church and this gave Colonel Smith had little choice but to surrender. According to Sir Alexander Denton *"..Those officers that commanded that place were taken and some 150 men, and some 19 killed on both sydes, the howse pilladged, all my cattell and wine taken away, my house the next day burnt down to the grounde and but one house left standinge in that end of the toune... "*.

The events at Hillesden are described in detail by Sir Samuel Luke.

"May it please your Excel^y
The last night after the Arivall of ye forces at Padbury Coll Cromwell sent out a p(ar)ty to give an Alarum at Hilsden Howse, which was p(er)formed, and wrought ye desired effect this morning between five and 6 of ye Clocke, they all Arrived before Hilsden Howse, and while Lieut General Cromwell, and maior generall Craford was putting ye forces in order ye howse sounded a parley, which was granted to them And Lieut generall Cromwell sent to them, and p(ro)mised to them a safe Conduct to any man ye they would send to treat: thereupon their brave Generall Coll Smith sent out to them his Lieut. Coll Curter, a dutchman, who demanded of us a safe Conduct with bagge and Baggage to Oxford, ye Quarter master General Vermuden was ordered by Lieut Generall to treat with him, who Assured him all they must expect was quarter, whereupon ye brave Lieu^t Coll returned, and in disdaine prepared for our Coming, we also prepared for an Assault. Ye Maior generall ordered ye foot to fall on in foure p^ts, which was done with ye brave resolution y^t I never saw anything better p(er)formed, in lesse than a quarter of an houres time, they made themselves masters of ye workes and howse, with the Losse of not above 6 men besides what were hurt on our side, and above 30 of theirs, in the howse we tooke Sr Alexander Denton, Coll Smith, with many other officers and souldiers, the number whereof is yet unknowne to us, we also tooke 13 barrell of powder with match and ball p(ro)portionable, ye Cellars full of good beere, ye Stables full of horses, and yards full of oxen and beastes, this hath ye Lord done for us this day his name for ever have ye honour and glory of it, we had no officer killed or hurt save onely Coll Pickering and ye onely a Little chocke under ye Chin with a musquet bullet but thankes be to god he was drest before I came away and was very

23

merry and chearfull, ye Lieut. general left 200 of Newport foot under Maior Bradbury in ye howse till he shall have further directions and they are all returned to their old quarters this night from whence they came, to wit: winslow,padbury, and other places thereabouts, the Enemies horse being abroad tooke some of ours, and we some of theirs and one a Captaine Walton (as I heare) was killed, thus begging leave to kisse your Excell. hand I rest

Newport 4th March,   *Your Excellency his*
1643 8 at night   *most humble servant*

Coll Smith Assured us they expected reliefe and therefore fired ye house this morning as if they intended to make a Burgaine Leaguer of it.

SAM. LUKE."[61]

The House was set on fire because news arrived on the 4th of March that a large body of royalist troops were advancing from Oxford. Rather than attempt to garrison Hillesden, with its incomplete defences, they destroyed the house and slighted the fortifications. Luke then withdrew to Newport Pagnell and Cromwell to Buckingham.

Hillesden today is a small village set on a low but very distinct hill, surmounted by the church. The House, which lay in the paddock immediately to the east of the church, had been rebuilt in 1648, but that building too has long since gone.[62] Today the site is just a pasture field. There is, not surprisingly, no sign of the relatively slight Civil War defences. It is however claimed that the numerous holes in the church door were caused by musket balls fired during the parliamentarian attack.

Pickering cannot have been commanding his regiment of foot in this engagement, for they were not embodied until 10 days later. He did not take up his command of the new regiment until

22 days after the storming of Hillesden House.[63] It is most likely that Pickering took part in the attack with his regiment of dragoons, brought up as part of the Eastern Association reinforcements.

Chapter 3

The Creation of the Regiment

In early April 1644 some Eastern Association dragoon companies were disbanded. This was because of a lack of volunteers and horses, and the poor quality of the troops that had been raised. Most of the men had been impressed into service. They were reduced into a single regiment under John Lilburne. It was presumably as a result of this reorganisation that Pickering relinquished command of his dragoons, which were said to have been *"a rude multitude."*[64]

On the 25th of March Pickering took command of one of the new infantry regiments that were being established in the second phase of expansion of the Eastern Association army.[65] The creation of the regiment during March and April can be traced from the surviving accounts.[66] There were 10 companies. The various company commanders took up their commissions between the 13th March and the 4th April 1644. In the succeeding days and weeks the companies were built up, though most never reached their full complement. The regiment was probably assembled in Cambridge, where it was mustered together with most of the rest of the army, in early April 1644.[67] Following Cambridge, the recorded musters of the army, from which regimental and company strength can be assessed, were held on the 8th May at Gainsborough, 23rd July at Doncaster and 18th September at St. Albans.[68] By the May muster Pickering's had reached its greatest strength, still only 738 men, although the regiment continued to recruit into July.[69] The composition of each company in 1644 is detailed in appendix II.

Only one reference to the colour of the regiment's flags has been traced, from October 1645, when mention is made of *"Colonel Pickering his Regiment of Blue, Colonell Hardresse Waller of Black, Colonell Montague's Regiment of Blue."*[70] This definitely refers to the colour of the flags not of the soldiers' coats. It was by their flags, or Colours, that many of the Civil War regiments were distinguished. This included, for example, the Red, Green and Orange regiments of the London Trained Bands and, later, the regiments of the New Model Army.[71] Although Markham states that a Colour should comprise the two principal colours of a commander's coat of arms, it is unclear whether such conventions were still being followed in the 1640s.[72] It was probably just coincidence that Pickering's Colours were blue while a blue lion was the principal device on the Pickering coat of arms.

No reference has yet been traced which shows the colour of the regimental coats.[73] The equipment of a regiment in the Eastern Association was supposed to be provided, in 1643-4, by the County Committee from which the new recruits were drawn. The coats were supplied by the Association. They were the only item of clothing which distinguished the soldiers of one regiment from those of another and by 1644 it was normally through the colour of the lining, rather than the colour of the coat itself, that the distinction was made.[74]

It is highly likely that Pickering's were equipped with red coats from the outset. This was the most common colour found in the Civil War armies and was apparently becoming the standard issue for Eastern Association regiments by 1644. Cromwell wrote to Mr. Russell, whose regiment had just been issued with red coats, saying: *"your troops refuse the new Coats. Say this: Wear them, or go home. I stand no more nonsense from any one. It is a needful thing we be as one in Colour; much ill having been from diversity of clothes, to slaying of friends by friends..."*[75] By the time Pickering's were incorporated into the New Model Army, red coats lined with blue were apparently becoming the norm.[76] There are various references to the purchase of red coats for the Eastern Association in 1644. The orders included red coats faced white for Colonel Montague's regiment and, for other unnamed regiments, red coats faced green, and red faced blue. The only exception are the green coats faced red.[77]

An idea of the costs of equipping the regiment can be gained from the records of purchases made for Pickering's and for other regiments at this time. The coats cost between about 9/6d and 11/- each.[78] Leather 'buff coats' cost up to three times that, and there is no reason to believe they were supplied to the common soldiers of Pickering's regiment.[79] Certainly by 1647 buff coats were seen solely as the uniform of a cavalry trooper or of an officer.[80] Shirts were also being purchased in April 1644 to supply the whole regiment.[81] Some of the equipment was second hand, for we find accounts in early April 1644 for the repair of muskets and other weapons.[82]

The absence of records of purchases of weapons and armour for Pickerings makes it impossible to be certain as to the exact equipment supplied to the regiment. This is because it was the county in which a regiment was raised that was expected to equip the soldiers. For this reason we cannot, for example, be certain that all the pikemen were issued with pikeman's armour, which was very expensive. The relative cost of the weapons and other equipment which the regiment would have required can be seen from general purchases in April 1644 for the Association:[83]

1000 muskets at 14/6d each
1000 swords and belts at 6/- each
1000 bandaleers at 17d each
400 pikes at 4/2d each
50 pikes at 5/- each
20 back, breeste and head peeces at 34/- each
8 drums at £10 total

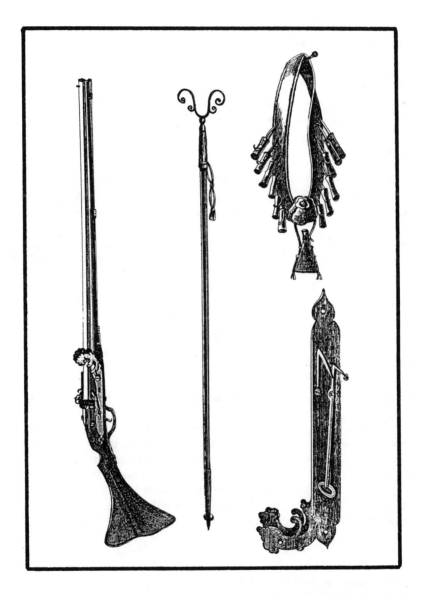

Figure 9 : Matchlock musket, with detail of lock mechanism, a rest and a bandolier, showing bullet bag, priming flask and powder flasks.

"Captine Silverwood his bill April the 12 1644

Willyam Di(..)n	for a worme sokit and mending the of his muskit 1/0d
Olever Holby	for mending the seare and spring of his muskit 0/4d
John Youing	for mending the seare and pan led of his muskit 0/6d
Willyam Warnes	for a kick pin and mending the pan led and tumbeler 0/8d
Thomas Estar	for a kock pin and mending and a spring mend the seare and tumbeller 1/0d
Robart tetell	for mending the kock and the tumbeller 0/6d
Thomas norman	for mending the tricker and the pan and seare 0/8d
John fullcher	for a seare a spring unbriching and dreling the tuch holl and mending the pan 1/10d
Thomas Lues	for a spring mending the seare and the pan 1/0d
Danill Sancrofft	for mending the pan and grifting into the barell 1/0d
Edmund dinnes	for mending the seare and the kock and spring 0/10d
Willyam Adames	for a tricker and mending the seare and spring 1/0d
Eievar fiske	for mending the tumbeller and the pan and pin to it 0/8d
Cristifor Goodwin	for a kockpin and a tricker and mending the seare 1/0d
John burdi	for a kockpin mending the pan led and seare 1/0d
Willyam bevarit	for a pan led pleating the stocke mending the (trenhard) 0/8d
Georg Fenar	for a new pan a rever a fleme a pin and mending the kock 2/2d
Willyam reake	for a new kockpin mending seare and spring 0/8d
Anthony Gibbon	for mending the seare and spring and panled 0/6d
Frances Breses	for mending seare tricker and spring 0/8d
James barallouf	for a new brichpin and mending the (vire) (r)eale(t) for the lock mending the seare 1/0d
Willyam Cross	for mending the lock of his miskit 0/4d
Richard gildarslese	for a new loupe and mending the spring and seare 1/0d

£1/0/0d

…. this worke done by me Edward Willarton
…….paid 19 April 1644"[84]

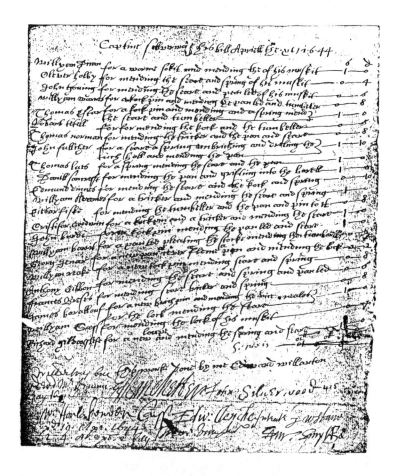

Figure 10 : Bill for the repair of muskets for Captain Silverwood's Company in April 1644. (Crown copyright)

Though Pickering originated from Titchmarsh in Northamptonshire, that county was not the recruiting ground for his regiment. Northamptonshire was part of the Midland Association. The Eastern Association consisted of the counties of

Figure 11 : The pikemen in Pickering's regiment were possibly issued with armour similar to, but less elaborate than this.

Norfolk, Suffolk, Essex, Cambridgeshire and the Isle of Ely, Lincolnshire, Huntingdonshire and Hertfordshire. Individual regiments of the Association were raised in specific parts of East Anglia. This was because Manchester believed that he could maintain an *esprit de corps* by drafting men from each county to keep up the regiment of that county. These recruiting grounds were generally maintained even after incorporation into the New Model Army in 1645.[85]

Most of the records of payment to Pickering's troops, other than those which came directly from the Association, refer to disbursements from the County Committee of Norfolk.[86] There are however also records of payments by the Suffolk Committee.[87] Most significant is the fact that in April 1645, just before the transfer of Pickering's into the New Model, some disturbances in Suffolk were caused by former soldiers of Pickering's regiment: "*by some old soldiers returned home, we have sent down to you Major Jubbes and Captain Axtell, two officers of Col.Pickering's regiment, to receive such soldiers as formerly belonged to that regiment.....If any other soldiers will come along with them and serve in that regiment these officers will take charge of them.*"[88] From this it is reasonable to conclude that Pickering's regiment was recruited in Suffolk and possibly in Norfolk. The men themselves were largely impressed into service and this was undoubtedly a major factor contributing to the high rate of desertion during 1644.

After August 1643, as part of the reorganisation of the Association, presumably under Cromwell's influence, commanders and officers for the regiments were chosen primarily for their military abilities, their godliness, discipline, and devotion to the parliamentarian cause. They were no longer normally drawn from the local gentry of the county within which the regiment was recruited. Instead the officers came from other parliamentarian armies or other regiments in the Association.

Figure 12 : The area of the Eastern Association.

34

	April 1644	Feb 1645	April 1645	1647	1649
Col	Pickering	Pickering	Pickering	Hewson	Hewson
Lt.C	Hewson	Hewson	Hewson	Jubbes	Axtell
Maj	Jubbes	Jubbes	Jubbes	Axtell	Carter
Capt	Axtell	Axtell	Axtell	Husbands now Grimes	Grimes
Capt	Husbands	Husbands	Husbands	Jenkins / Tomkins / Toppington	Gayle
Capt	Jenkins	Jenkins	Jenkins	Carter	Brafield
Capt	Cromwell	Cromwell	Silverwood	Silverwood	Axtell
Capt	Carver	Karver	Carter	was Gayle	Atkinson
Capt	Silverwood	Silverwood	Gale	Price	Smith
Capt	Ware	Carter	Price		Jenkins

Table 1 : Senior Officers of the Regiment[89]

A Colonel did not take full responsibility for the command of a regiment, he was in many respects a general officer. This was after all Pickering's military background, having come into the Association, following diplomatic work, to serve as Commissary General for the Musters. Much of the responsibility for the command of a regiment fell upon the Lieutenant Colonel. It is therefore not surprising to find that, unlike Pickering, Hewson had more than a year's experience as a Company commander before he took up his commission as Lieutenant Colonel in Pickering's regiment. John Hewson had been a shoemaker in the capital, who sold to the Massachusetts Company before the war. According to Wood, Hewson was "*Sometime an honest shoemaker in Westminster, but getting little by the trade, he in the beginning of*

35

the grand rebellion, went out as a captain upon the account of the blessed cause..."[90] He had served as a captain in the Earl of Essex's own regiment from late 1642, and joined Pickering's on the 26th March 1644.[91]

John Jubbes' family lived in Norwich.[92] He had joined the Eastern Association army as a Captain of foot in Colonel Sir Miles Hubbard's regiment at its formation, on the 14th April 1643. Jubbes had, in his own words, joined the army because he "had been long deeply sensible of the many greevous Incroachments and Usurpations excercised over the People of this Nation."[93] He may have seen action with the regiment at the siege of Crowland in 1643 and in the other engagements of the Association in Lincolnshire in the same year.[94] Captain Jubbes left Hubbard's regiment to take up his commission as Major with Pickering's regiment on the 16th March 1644 and it seems, from the frequency with which he distributed money to the companies in 1644, that he had some special financial responsibility within the regiment.[95]

Before joining Pickering's, Jubbes had also collected money in Norfolk, Suffolk and Essex for the army. Manchester had appointed army officers as commissioners to reassess the 'taxes' called the Fifth and the Twentieth, though later it was a task fulfilled by civilian officials.[96] Jubbes recorded in his Account that he was due "other moneys for my extraordinary serveses due by myself and servants and horses upon raising of moneys upon the fith and twentieth part in the Countys of Norfolk, Suffux and Essex by order from the Earl of Manchester the care of which three countys was referred wholly unto me in cheife....."[97]

In a letter, dated 10th December 1643, Thomas Windham wrote : "My personal estate I have given up at two thousand pounds, which is one more than I know I am worth, my estate in lands to the uppermost, during my father's life. The oppression practised by Jubs and his associates is very odious, their fury in churches detestable...."[98] Ketton-Cremer argues that "Lt.Col.John

Jubbes who expressed violently anti-monarchical sentiments at the critical Army Council of 1st November 1647.... was just the kind of man to display detestable fury in churches". He believes that this was "*random iconoclasm, carried out by local puritan extremists or detachments of unruly troops.*"[99] This is far from the truth. The 'Solemn League and Covenant' signed between Parliament and the Scots required the reformation of religion in England and Ireland in doctrine, discipline, and government. In other words, a presbyterian form of church government was to be imposed. In August 1643 an ordinance was passed for "*the utter demolishing, removing and taking away of all monuments of superstition and idolatry*", and in December a systematic implementation was ordered. This raised the opposition of many 'moderate' parliamentarians and puritans, such as Windham. However, he had also been accused of undervaluing his estate when a levy was made in 1643 to raise money for the war. It is in the context of this matter of taxation that we should understand Windham's letter of accusation. Jubbes was certainly not one of Ketton-Cremer's "*unruly troopers.*"

Daniel Axtell had been a Lieutenant in Essex's army and joined Pickering's as first captain on the 18th March 1644.[100] Unlike Pickering, Axtell's religious background was as a baptist. He was one of a number of baptists, including Lilburne and Overton, of humble and obscure origins who rose to positions of influence through the New Model Army.[101]

Azariah Husbands had been a cornet in Essex's army before joining Pickering's, on 15th March 1644, as second captain.[102] Grimes replaced Husbands at some time between April 1645 and 1647.[103] John Jenkins joined Pickering's as third captain on 4th April 1644, but was killed at Faringdon in April 1645.[104] He was succeeded by Captain Tomkins, a Welshman, who was killed at Naseby two months later. Tomkins was replaced in his turn by Toppington, previously Lieutenant to Hewson.[105] Cromwell joined the regiment as fourth captain on 13th March 1644 but did not transfer with Pickering's into the New Model in 1645. It is possible that he was promoted to a higher position in another regiment, though there may equally have been religious and political reasons for his leaving.[106] There is no evidence of family association with Oliver Cromwell. Carver joined the regiment on

Figure 13 : Edward Montague, later Earl of Sandwich, in 1642 at the age of 17. A friend of John Pickering, he commanded an Eastern Association infantry regiment from the autumn of 1643.

the 15th March 1644 as fifth captain. John Silverwood took up his commission as sixth captain on the 18th March.[107] Ware became the seventh captain on the 17th March. He was also later replaced, in February 1645, by John Carter. Reynold Gayle joined the regiment in 1644 as captain lieutenant in Pickering's own company and was raised to captain of the 7th company in April 1645 but was killed at Bristol in the same year.[108] The earlier history of Price, who became a captain in April 1645, has not been established.[109]

Within the Association the regiments were grouped into brigades. During the 1644 campaign Pickering's regiment were in Crawford's brigade. Laurence Crawford, Major General of the Eastern Association, was born in Scotland in 1611. An experienced and courageous commander, Crawford had served under Gustavus Adolphus in the German wars from 1629. After the battle of Lutzen he returned home to command a regiment that Charles I sent to suppress the Irish rebellion in 1641.[110]

Fighting in Crawford's brigade alongside John Pickering's was the regiment of his friend Edward Montague. Edward was born at Barnwell, Northamptonshire, in 1625, the son of Sir Sidney Montague who was a relation of the Earl of Manchester. He was brought up at Hinchingbrooke House, Cambridgeshire, which his father had bought from the Cromwells. The Pickerings and the Montagues were linked in marriage, for Edward's sister had married John's elder brother and although Sir Sidney Montague was a royalist, Edward fought for parliament. After the war, through Cromwell's patronage, he received considerable advancement to become a Lord, a Councillor of State and Admiral of the English fleet. His allegiance was presumably, first and foremost, to Oliver Cromwell and it was only after the Protector's death, at the time of Booth's Rising in 1659, that Edward transferred his support to the king. He travelled to the continent to meet Charles II and was one of those instrumental in the restoration of the king in 1660. In recognition of his service to Charles II Edward Montague was created the first Earl of Sandwich.[111]

At Marston Moor Crawford's brigade comprised Pickering's, Montague's, Crawford's and Russell's regiments. Pickering's and Montague's had much in common, particularly in religion and together with Major General Skippon's regiment, they were later described as "*ye preaching and praying regiments.*"[112] The strong puritan religious beliefs of many of Manchester's commanders is well known. Russell and Montague, for example, were described in 1644 as "*those two valiant religious colonels.*"[113]

RANK/OFFICE	DAILY PAY
Colonel (and as Captain)	£2/05/00
Lt.Colonel (and as Captain)	£1/10/00
Major (and as Captain)	£1/04/00
Captain	£0/15/00
Provost Marshall*[114]	£0/05/00
Quartermaster*[115]	£0/05/00
Lieutenant(second in command of company)	£0/04/00
Surgeon*	£0/04/00
Ensign(third in command of company)	£0/03/00
Wagoner*	£0/03/00
Surgeon's mate*	
Sergeant[116] (ideally 3 per company)	£0/01/06
Gentleman at Arms[117]	£0/01/06
Clerk[118] (1 per company)	£0/01/06
Corporal[119] (ideally 3 per company)	£0/01/00
Gentleman of the Company[120]	£0/01/00
Drum major[121]	£0/01/00
Drum (ideally 2 per company)	£0/01/00
private soldier	£0/00/08

(* Staff officers of the regiment)

Table 2 : Composition and pay of the regiment[122]

Chapter 4

The Campaigns of 1644

Lincoln, Sleaford and Crowland had all been captured by the Earl of Manchester in October 1643, but in March 1644 they had been retaken by Prince Rupert. As Lincolnshire was by now part of the Eastern Association, Manchester's forces were committed to retrieve the situation. The army was then to advance into Yorkshire, where Fairfax's Northern army and the Scots had driven the Royalists back into their garrison at York. A detailed record of the route followed during the 1644 campaigns is provided by Colonel Montague's journal (Appendix I). As his regiment was in the same brigade, this journal provides a guide to the movements of Pickering's regiment, although it is probable that the two regiments were not always quartered in the same places.

After the storming of Hillesden House, Montague's regiment, with others from Crawford's brigade, returned to Newport Pagnell. There they remained in garrison for about 11 weeks. At this time Pickering's new regiment was being assembled, and in early April it was mustered at Cambridge. The quarters used by Pickering's appear to have been at Histon, three miles to the north of the city.[123]

On the 20th April Manchester's army, including Pickering's, was assembled at Huntingdon. They then marched north towards Lincoln via Oundle, Stamford and Grantham. Undoubtedly Pickering took the opportunity, while the army was at Oundle, to visit his family at Titchmarsh. Perhaps the regiment even quartered there during the night of the 22nd April. Montague certainly seems to have stopped at his former home village, Barnwell, just a few miles to the north.

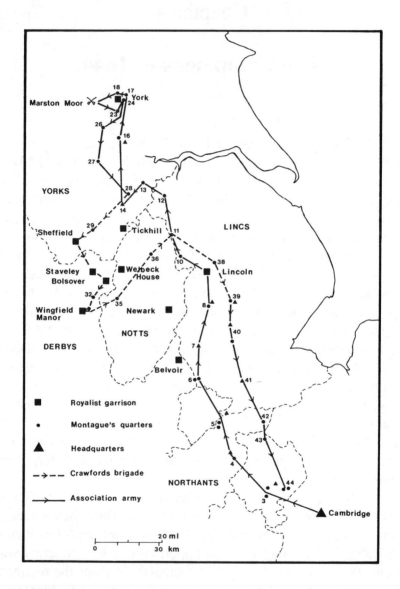

Figure 14 : Map of the Marston Moor campaign, based on Colonel Montague's journal. (For key to numbered places see Appendix I).

The army reached Lincoln by the 3rd of May.[124] The Association army was at first drawn up overlooking Lincoln, on the brow of a hill near Canwick, about a mile south of the city. The core of the city's defences were the embattled Medieval wall of the Cathedral Close together with the castle. This was the upper town. It sat high on the hill overshadowing the rest of the city, which lay to the south, on slopes down to the river, with the suburbs on the valley floor beyond. The lower town was defended by the old city wall, with other Medieval outworks beyond, protecting the southern suburbs. Although he did not get the support he had wished from Prince Rupert, Sir Francis Fane's royalist garrison in the Close was *"well manned with 2000 men and good store of provisions and ammunition"*.

Previously, in 1643, the city had changed hands twice without a shot being fired. This time the parliamentarians had to resort to force of arms. On the night of Thursday 2nd, according to a royalist source, the garrison *"killed threescore of the rebels who came near the works"*. The assault on the main defences planned for Saturday 4th May was abandoned due to the very muddy conditions caused by continuous rain. It was *"so slippery it was not possible for our foot to crawl up the hill to come to their works..."* On Monday the 6th, before dawn, the attack was finally mounted. At the firing of six parliamentarian cannon Montague's and Russell's regiments attacked the gate and drawbridge. Within a quarter of an hour Manchester's forces had taken the lower town. The defenders retreated up the hill to the castle and the Cathedral Close.

In the morning the final assault began. Though it was a steep ascent through the lower to the upper town, the buildings along the streets would have provided good cover. An easier approach would have been possible from the north and east across level ground outside the defences but here there would have been little cover. As the parliamentarians approached the fortifications

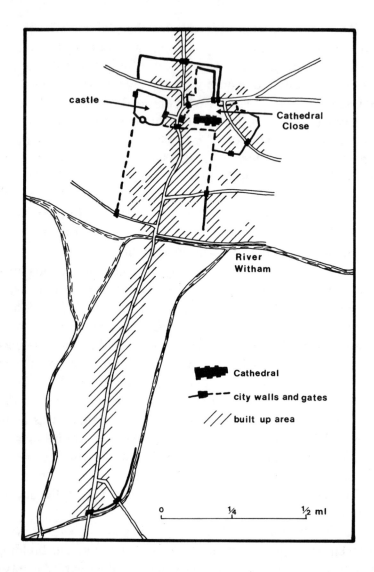

Figure 15 : Lincoln circa 1610. The layout of the Civil War defences which supplemented the surviving Medieval defences has not been determined. (After Speed and also Hill)

Figure 16 : Lincoln Cathedral from the south east in 1803, showing the remains of the wall of the Cathedral Close and the Potter Gate.

they were met by the royalists with shot "*which they poured out like haile*" but, with "*every Division beating back the Enemy*", they soon reached the walls. They then set up scaling ladders against the defences, although many of the ladders were too short for the high walls. The royalists, using pikes, pushed the attackers back and fired pistols and carbines. The assault seems to have had much of the character of a Medieval siege, for there was no softening up of the defences with artillery. The parliamentarians simply scaled the walls as the defenders seized the ladders and threw down great stones, "*by which we received more hurt than by*

45

all their shot." However *"the enemy... had no spirit now left in them, but betook themselves to their heeles from the walls..."*[125] Within an hour the royalists in the Cathedral Close and the castle had surrendered.

In all about 50 were killed during the assault, 20 of these in the attack on the Castle where there was the greatest resistance. The whole of Crawford's brigade, including Pickering's, were involved in the assault, for it was later said of Colonel Pickering that *"his gallantry at the storming of Lincoln Close is known to many."*[126] According to Montague, 50 officers and between 700 or 800 soldiers were taken prisoner during the assault, a further 60 killed and *"all theire greate Guns Cariages Armes and Ammunicion"* captured.[127] Not surprisingly, with a wealthy city like Lincoln, the plundering, which was allowed in the upper town, proved very profitable to the parliamentarian soldiers.

Today there are still extensive ruins of the castle, which was the focus of the most intense fighting during the siege. It is now a park open to the public. In the 19th century the walls were restored to their original height, giving one a feeling for the daunting task that had faced the Association forces who assaulted the castle. Standing before these massive defences one must agree with the parliamentarian account which describes *"the Mount whereon the Castle stood, being near as steep as the eaves of a house."* The Medieval Potter Gate and the Roman Newport Arch, which both controlled access to the Cathedral Close, the Lower West Gate to the town and fragments of the town walls also survive. They give a good idea of the scale of the defences that Pickering's had to scale in the assault on the Cathedral Close, though they are nowhere as formidable as the defences of the castle.

On the 8th May the Association army marched north, leaving Palgrave's regiment to hold Lincoln. The siege of York had begun on the 20th April with Fairfax's forces and the Earl of

Figure 17 : A view from the south eastern defences of York circa 1875, showing the scale of the Medieval defences.

Leven's 16,000 strong Scottish army facing the city. Fairfax had appealed to the Earl of Manchester for assistance as there was no sign of the royalist garrison surrendering. The Association army advanced via Torksey to Gainsborough, crossing the Trent on a bridge of boats. By the 21st they approached Doncaster. The weather was appalling, making the transporting of heavy artillery and supplies extremely difficult. As a result the advance was slow and, although it was only an 80 mile journey, they did not arrive at York until the 3rd June.[128]

The Association army sealed the northern circuit of the city while Fairfax controlled the east and Leven the south and west. The Earl of Manchester established his headquarters near Clifton, to the north west of the city. A general attack on the 6th of June

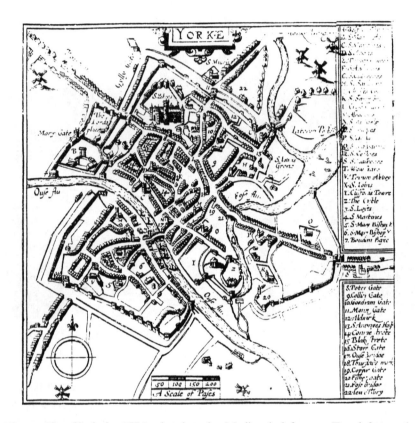

Figure 18 : York in 1574, showing the Medieval defences. Top left are the Bootham Bar (7), and Manor House Garden (The Lords Place) with St.Mary's Tower at its north west corner.

forced the royalists from the suburbs and brought Manchester's troops within reach of the city walls. The Earl then raised a battery outside the Bootham Bar, the northern gate to the city, only 40 yards from the wall. For many days they dug a mine under the adjacent St.Mary's tower, from houses just outside the defences. At the same time Fairfax's men undermined Walmgate Bar. A parley on the 15th of June was unsuccessful, but by the 16th the

Figure 19 : The Bootham Bar, York, as it was in the late 19th century.

mines were completed. It had been intended that feigned attacks be mounted around the town as the mines were sprung. Early in the morning the Association cannon demolished part of the wall immediately south of St.Mary's Tower, and the mine was fired causing the tower itself to collapse. But Crawford had attacked prematurely, without advising the other commanders, and therefore there was no diversionary action.

About 600 of Crawford's brigade entered through the breach and scaled the inner walls with ladders, getting into the garden and bowling green of the Manor. A parliamentarian account records that "*the bold soldiers adventured too farre through inconsiderateness, and hope of plunder, many of them having scaled two or three inner walles, posessed themselves of the Mannor.*" Because of the absence of other attacks, the brigade was met by perhaps as many as two thousand of Newcastle's white coats and a company of volunteer citizens. As a result they suffered heavy losses. A party of royalists came out through a sally port and entered the Manor via the breach, closing off the brigade's only retreat. With most of their powder and shot gone they had to surrender.

Crawford lost about 250 taken prisoner, about 100 wounded and 40 killed. The royalist losses may also have been large, for it was claimed that they lost two Colonels and a Lieutenant Colonel, implying that many ordinary soldiers were also killed. It is known that Montague's regiment was heavily involved in the attack, but it is unclear what role Pickering's played. The siege of York was intentionally passed over in Pickering's obituary, unlike the praise for his attack at Lincoln, and this would suggest that Pickering's were involved. It was probably felt that the attack on the Manor had been such a disastrous failure that it should not be described.[129] It was to be the only significant engagement while the parliamentarian armies lay before York. On the 30th June the parliamentarians were forced to lift the siege because of the approach of Prince Rupert, who was advancing with a substantial force to relieve the city.

Today the defences of York remain intact throughout most of the circuit of the city. This includes the western defences faced by Manchester's forces. The Bootham Bar, repaired and refaced in the late 1640s, is still impressive. The wall of the manor also survives and, on the nearby St. Mary's tower, the later repairs to the section of the tower that was destroyed in the siege are still clearly visible. It is said that bullets from the fierce fighting in the manor grounds have been found within the Manor walls.[130]

On the morning of Tuesday 2nd July 1644 the combined forces of the Northern and the Eastern Associations and the Scots met the army of Prince Rupert and the Earl of Newcastle near Long Marston village. The field of battle was Marston Moor, just eight miles to the west of York. This was to prove one of the most decisive battles of the Civil War. Whoever won was likely to control York and therefore much of northern England.

Pickering's, together with most of the Association foot were on the left wing of the army. Immediately to their left were the Association horse under Cromwell. Fairfax's and the Scottish forces in the centre and on the right were soon halted in their advance onto the Moor and were then pushed back. The Association foot under Crawford, with Cromwell's horse, were more successful. In this initial attack, Crawford's brigade were opposed by O'Niell's regiment.[131] "*Upon the advancing of the Earle of Manchester's foot, after short firing on both sides, we caused the enemy to quit the hedge in a disorderly manner.*"[132] Thereafter they "*did very good execution*", passing out onto the Moor at "*a running march*", the foot and horse together sweeping across the battlefield carrying almost all before them. Crawford did meet resistance from Rupert's foot who, "*standing soe stoutly to it*" caused "*most of Manchester's blew coats wth fought under the bloody colours*" to be killed.[133]

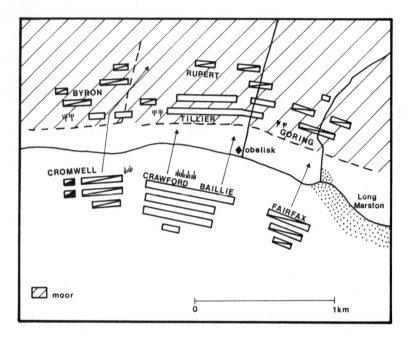

Figure 20 : The battle of Marston Moor (after Smurthwaite & Newman)

Finally Crawford advanced against Newcastle's own regiment of Whitecoats, as they made their famous last stand in White Syke Close. After the battle Crawford's brigade were singled out from the rest of the infantry for particular praise: *"Monday we had further intelligence of the fight neere York, and of the gallant performance of Colonell Cromwell and his horse, ...and how the Brigade consisting of Col.Russel, Col.Montague and Col.Pickerings regiments behaved themselves most gallantly."*[134] As another newsheet reported, *"What should I name the Brigade of Col.Russell, Col.Montague, and Col.Pickering, who stood as a wall of Brasse....."*[135]

On the 4th July the triumphant parliamentarian forces returned to York and summoned the city to surrender. With all chance of relief now gone, on the 11th the royalists consented to a parley and on the 16th the garrison marched out of the city. Although the royalist forces were given safe passage from York, some parliamentarians plundered the enemy baggage. These events were discussed at a Council of War on Thursday 25th July, and a team was appointed to investigate the event.[136] They included Pickering and Jubbes.

From York the Association army marched south on the 20th July. Following the destruction of the king's northern army at Marston Moor, the Earl of Manchester was free to clear the royalists from the East Midlands. Although he had suffered substantial losses, Manchester still commanded a formidable army which none of the local royalist forces could hope to defeat. While the army was at Doncaster, Welbecke House surrendered. At the same time Tickhill Castle was summoned and taken by Lilburne, against the instructions of the Earl of Manchester.[137] It seems unlikely that Pickering's or Montague's were involved in either action, although of this we cannot be certain.[138]

On the 1st August three regiments were detached from the main army and detailed for the reduction of the royalist garrisons of south Yorkshire and north Derbyshire. The brigade, under the command of Major General Crawford, comprised Crawford's, Montague's and Pickering's regiments, the latter for the moment without its Colonel. In all the brigade numbered no more than one thousand men, a clear indication of the serious effect the campaign was having on the army. They were accompanied by Lieutenant Colonel Rich's troops and Colonel Sidney's regiment of horse.[139] From Doncaster and the surrounding villages they marched via Conisborough, the foot halting for the night at Rotherham, and then on the following day to Sheffield. In that town a royalist garrison held the Medieval castle, which lay at the north east corner of the town, at the junction of the rivers Don and Sheaf. The garrison, under the command of Major Beaumont, consisted of some 200 foot and a troop of horse. The castle was "*strongly fortified with a broad and deep Trench of 18 ft. deep, and water in it, a strong brest-work Pallizadoed, a wall round of 2 yards thick, eight peices of Iron-ordinance and 2 Morter-pieces. Our forces being come neere this Castle, sent then three great shot, which did execution in the Castle, after which they sent a Summons to the Castle, who shot three times at the trumpeter... and they flourished their Swords cryed out they would have no other parley.*"

The next step was to set up artillery before the castle. Two batteries were erected within 30 yards of the outworks and on the 5th August the bombardment began. After twenty-four hours it was realised that the demi-culverin was having little effect. They therefore sent for a culverin, called the 'Queen's Pocket Pistol'. This siege piece made quick work of the Medieval defences. As Montague recorded, the bombardment lasted until the 10th, "*in wch tyme wee made 468 greate shott against the Castle....*" By then the cannon had "*brought the strong walls thereof down into the trenches and made a perfect breach.*" A parley followed in which Pickering was one of the commissioners. On the 11th the garrison agreed terms and were allowed to march out. At Sheffield the brigade captured "*400 Armes, 12 barrels of powder, much Match, 20 tuns of yron-shot, about £400 worth of Corne, Beefe, Bacon, Cheese etc, the Countrey people thereabouts, voluntarily gathering and giving to his souldiers, at least £500 as a gratuity for this good services...*"

Sheffield castle was demolished in 1648 and today almost all trace has gone. The whole site is now part of the commercial heart of the city and the only significant reminders of the castle are several road names such as Castle Gate and Castle Street.[140]

On the 12th August the brigade marched south to Staveley, Mr.John Fretchwell's house. It had been garrisoned for the king in the spring of 1644 and was strongly fortified. However, the governor gave up the house without a shot being fired, apparently under instruction from the owner. Fretchwell had been captured at Marston Moor or had surrendered at York. He had agreed to lay down his arms and to order his house to surrender in return for Fairfax's protection.[141]

The house stands immediately north of the church. It was remodelled in the 18th and 19th century but the Fretchwell coat of arms still dominates the porch. It is in a commanding position on the north edge of Staveley, the ground falling away on the north, west and east. The surrounding landscape has been heavily industrialised, while extensive landscaping around the house in later centuries has probably removed all trace of the Civil War defences. There are however some slight earthworks of uncertain significance, in a paddock on the slope to the north east side of the house, which may be the remnants of fortifications.

On the 13th Crawford marched on to Bolsover, just 4 miles to the south east. Before this landscape was urbanised and vast spoil heaps from the coal mining raised in the valley, Bolsover Castle would have been clearly visible from Staveley. The castle was the Earl of Newcastle's main residence. The splendour of the house is clear even today, though no longer occupied and partly ruined, reflecting the great wealth of the Earl in the 17th century. It stands in an impressive and commanding position on a small spur running westwards from the high ridge occupied by the town. It is an impressive property, in the care of English Heritage and retains many of the buildings which existed in 1644.

Although in a strong defensive position and retaining the core of its Medieval defensive walls, it was by this time a mansion not a castle. The 'Little Castle', a complete house in its own right, was an early 17th century romantic folly rather than a Medieval keep. The main house was the long terrace range seen facing to the right on figure 21. The castle had been garrisoned for the king in the spring of 1644. It was held by Colonel Muschamp and was

Figure 21 : Bolsover Castle in 1787 viewed from the west. The 'Little Castle' is in the centre. The Terrace Court, which was in the 17th century the main house, is seen to the right.

" *well manned with souldiers, and strengthened with Great guns... and it had strong works about it...* " It is likely that the Brigade faced the castle on the east side, on the level ground towards the town, for on all the other sides the steep scarps would have made approach very difficult. Despite its strong defensive position, the castle only resisted for a single day. It yielded on the 14th without the need for a costly assault. The royalist troops marched out on the 15th with drums and colours, horses, swords and pistols, but leaving behind them six pieces of ordnance and 300 firearms. The castle was then garrisoned by parliamentarian troops, a garrison that was maintained throughout the Civil War, only being abandoned in 1649.[142]

Figure 22 : The sumptuous interior of the 'Little Castle' at Bolsover. This fanciful Victorian drawing may reflect the reality of some successful sieges for Pickering's.

On the 17th the brigade marched the nine miles to Wingfield Manor. This garrison had changed hands several times, but now comprised 300 royalist troops under Colonel Molyneux. Colonel Gell and Lord Grey, who commanded the parliamentarian forces in the region, had taken the victory at Marston Moor as a sign to move against royalist garrisons in the East Midlands. Wingfield was a major objective. Montague wrote, on the 21st we *"faced Wingfeild Mannor with our regiments were Sir John Gell had beleagured the same a monnth before."* The combined forces

Figure 23 : The ruins of Wingfield Manor, Derbyshire, as they were in 1823.

of Gell and Crawford, with the latter's effective siege artillery, made short work of the garrison. The artillery was moved within 400 yards of the walls and within three hours a large breach was created. According to Montague, "*after some few great shott*" had been fired against the castle the governor sounded a parley. As so often, Pickering was a commissioner and, with the negotiations successfully concluded, the garrison marched out on the 21st.

The earthen Civil War outworks are not visible but the impressive ruins of the 15th century fortified house at Wingfield Manor still survive. They lie in open countryside about a mile to the west of South Wingfield village. It is an impressive ruin set on a spur, with ground sloping steeply away on three sides.[143]

The brigade returned to Gainsborough on the 24th *August* "*where now we remaine not six men fewer then when we left*

58

Doncaster, onely some few are sickened."[144] There was no obvious challenge in the region now to Manchester's army and he could have continued the campaign by tackling other important royalist strongholds. Pickering later claimed the army had intelligence that the garrison of Newark was in a weak state, divided and fearful of a siege. He, Cromwell and Ireton had apparently urged Manchester to attack Newark immediately. The Earl had already opposed the taking of Tickhill Castle, which only fell because Lilburne had ignored his instructions. Manchester again disregarded his officers' advice and retreated with the whole army to Lincoln. Here he argued against an attack on Belvoir Castle and other nearby royalist garrisons. These sites were an obvious threat to the Association and had the Earl taken them he might have secured the whole region for parliament. However, this major opportunity was lost and the Newark and Belvoir garrisons continued to provide a threat throughout the rest of the war.

On the 3rd of September Manchester received orders from the Committee of Both Kingdoms to take his army into the south west. He therefore marched from Lincoln, reaching Huntingdon on the 7th, where it was intended to muster and pay the troops. However orders arrived for the army to move rapidly into action, because the Earl of Essex's army had been defeated in Cornwall. Again Manchester was unwilling to act decisively. According to Pickering, the Earl wished instead that his forces be quartered in St.Albans rather than march, as he had been instructed, to Dorchester and Abingdon. In early October they were still at Reading. After further vacillation the army, comprising some 5000 horse and foot and 24 cannon, finally advanced once more.[145]

The main royalist garrison in the Newbury area was at Donnington Castle. The fortifications of this small Medieval stone castle had been strengthened with a new earthen curtain, with massive diamond shaped bastions, surrounded by a deep ditch. Such outworks, with turf revetting and timber palisadoes, were far

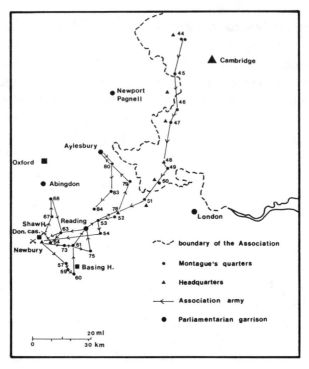

Figure 24 : The Newbury campaign. (Key to numbered places see Appendix I).

less vulnerable to artillery bombardment than Medieval stone walls. They also provided an effective artillery platform. Today only the gatehouse of the Medieval castle still stands, scarred by the artillery bombardment of the siege, but it is surrounded by well preserved earthworks of the Civil War defences.[146]

Colonel Horton had begun the siege of Donnington Castle on the 29th September but, despite a 12 day barrage, the garrison refused to yield. When Manchester's army reached Newbury, on the 6th October, they joined the siege. In addition to artillery fire the parliamentarians now started mining on the opposite side of the castle. In response the garrison launched a strong sally against the besieging force. It is unclear whether Pickering's saw any action.

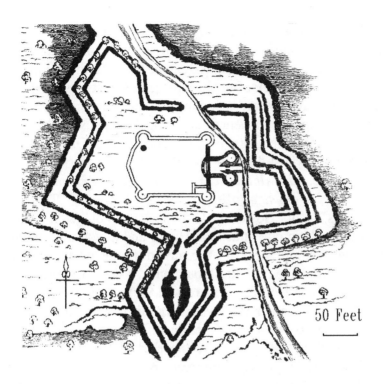

50 Feet

Figure 25 : 19th century plan of Civil War earthworks around Donnington Castle.

Montague makes no mention of any fighting while they were at Newbury, between the 6th and 17th, so the brigade may not have been involved. Horton's artillery had shattered three of the castle towers, but the siege did not continue long enough to enable the parliamentarians to take advantage of this. Already by the 8th October the king was at Shaftesbury, marching east with a relieving force of 5500 foot and 4000 horse. On the 15th October he had advanced to Salisbury, just 30 miles away. In response, Waller's, Essex's and Manchester's forces were ordered to unite at Basing. Therefore, on the 17th, after just ten days, Manchester had to draw off from Donnington Castle.[147]

They reached Basingstoke on the same day, where a Committee met which selected the battle formation in the event that they were drawn into an engagement.[148] At the same time Crawford made a survey of the royalist garrison at Basing House, which was besieged by forces drawn from the Southern Associated Counties. He expressed a belief that it could be quickly taken if he were given reinforcements of just 1000 men. On the 19th, according to a royalist diary of the siege, "*eight regiments of foot and some horse, with all their carriage and artillery (were) drawn on the south of Basingstoke facing the House.*"[149] This was Manchester's army. However, Crawford did not get his wish. There was no attempt to attack the House and it would be another twelve months before Pickering's returned. By then they were part of the New Model Army and would play a decisive role in the storming of Basing House.[150] The reason for the withdrawal on the night of the 19th October 1644 was that Manchester had to support Waller's retreat to Basingstoke. It was at Basingstoke on the 21st October that they were joined by the Earl of Essex and by this time Manchester's army, reinforced by other troops, which included some 5000 infantry of the London Trained Bands, comprised about 7000 horse and 7000 foot.[151]

The parliamentarian forces advanced to Thackham. This forced the king to defend Newbury, "*hoping that, upon the advantage he had of the Town of Newbury and the River, the Enemy would not speedily Advance; and that in the mean time, by being compell'd to lodge in the Field, which grew now to be very Cold, whilst his Army was under cover, they might be forced to retire.*" The royalist army was deployed around the town. "*The greatest part of the Army was placed towards the Enemies Quarters, in a good House belonging to Mr. Doleman at Shaw, and in a village near it, defended by the river that runs under*

Donnington Castle, and in a House between that village and Newbury, about which a Work was cast up, and at a Mill upon the River of Kennet..." [152] The horse and artillery stood in two open fields to the north, while Prince Maurice's foot and some horse were in Speen village to the west. Manchester's artillery and foot were on Clay Hill, north east of Newbury, facing Shaw House.

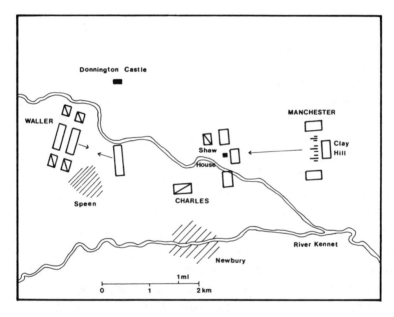

Figure 26 : The second battle of Newbury, 1644.

The parliamentarians attacked on the 28th of October, in what was the second battle of Newbury.[153] There is no specific mention of Pickering's in the accounts of the battle, but they were certainly present at Newbury[154] and they were presumably still part of Crawford's brigade, together with Montague's regiment which we know was involved throughout.[155] Manchester seems to have committed all his infantry to the attack.

From what we know of Pickering's, it seems likely that they were one of the regiments which, in the attack, "*came singing of Psalms.*" Events were not to go well for the Association. The horse and foot under Skippon, Cromwell, Waller and Balfour advanced from the south west of Donnington and attacked the royalists at Speen, with notable success. It was not however until two hours later that "*...twelve hundred horse, and three thousand foot, of those under the earl of Manchester, advanced with great resolution upon Shaw-House, and the Field adjacent; which quarter was defended by Sr Jacob Astley, and Colonel George Lisle; and the House by Lieutenant Colonel Page. They came singing of Psalms; and, at first, drove forty Musqueteers from a Hedge, who were placed there to stop them; but they were presently Charg'd by Sr John Brown with the Prince's Regiment of horse; who did good execution upon them, till he saw another Body of their horse ready to charge him, which made him retire to the foot in Mr Doleman's garden, which flanked that Field, and give fire upon those horse, whereof very many fell; and the horse thereupon Wheeling about, Sr John Brown fell upon the Rear, kill'd many, and kept that ground all the day; when the Reserve of foot, commanded by Colonel Thelwell, gall'd their foot with several Vollies; and then fell on them with the But-ends of their Musquets, till they had not only beaten them from the Hedges, but quite out of the Filed; leaving two Drakes, some Colours, and many dead Bodies behind them. At this time, a great Body of their foot attempted Mr Doleman's House, but were so well entertain'd by Lieutenant Colonel Page, that after they had made their first effort, they were forced to retire in such Confusion, that he pursu'd them from the House with a notable Execution; insomuch that they left five hundred dead upon a little spot of ground; and they drew off the two Drakes out of the Filed to the House, the Enemy being beaten off, and retired from all that Quarter.*" In contrast, the parliamentarians had the upper hand in the action at Speen, but did not continue their advance. It was however a moonlight night and *"that part of the Enemy that had been so roughly treated at Shaw, having receiv'd Soccour of a strong Body of horse, resolv'd once more to make an attempt upon the foot there; but they were beaten off as before; though they stood not well enough to receive an equal loss, but retired to their Hill, where they stood still."*[156]

Figure 27 : The Elizabethan mansion of Shaw House, Newbury, early this century.

Shaw House, the scene of the only significant defeat in which Pickering's were ever involved, still survives today, as a school. It is the largest Elizabethan mansion in Berkshire, and looks today very much as it did in 1644. However, the surrounding landscape has changed dramatically in the intervening centuries. According to Gaunt, an *"ancient earthwork"* exists around Shaw House, but it is unclear whether this is a remnant of Civil War defences. No reference is made to defences around the House in the contemporary accounts.[157]

Figure 28 : The ruined gatehouse of Donnington Castle in the 18th century. Civil War earthworks are visible in the foreground.

It is generally considered that the parliamentarians had the worst of the action. Clarendon for example wrote: "*there could be no question there were many more kill'd of the Enemy, than of the King's Army...*"[158] However this may not have been the feeling in Manchester's army, for Montague recorded: "*Wee fought with the kings Armye lyeing in Shaw and Newbery and Dinnington Castle, and drove them out of the Townes were wee tooke 356 Prisoners with the Earle of Cleveland and the Lady Rutham 7 ffield Pieces the kinge flyeinge towards Bath wth 10 men only.*" The parliamentarians were in control of Newbury and Shaw House and returned, on the 31st October, to lay siege to Donnington Castle.

The governor of the royalist garrison, Sir John Boys, would not consider surrender. A weak attempt was made to storm the castle but it was repulsed and on the 2nd November the siege was lifted again. The king relieved the castle on the evening of the 9th, bringing in new supplies and taking away the artillery that had been left there after the battle. It seemed likely that a third battle was about to take place. The parliamentarian foot were drawn up behind hedges just to the west of Shaw House and there were skirmishes that night. On the 10th Manchester marched into the field after the retreating royalists but there was no fight.

The king might well have won any such engagement, for he had taken up a position close to the castle. The Association forces had already been fired upon by the artillery in the castle on the 7th and they would have been under similar cannon fire on the battlefield. Moreover, the parliamentarian army had been severely weakened by the Newbury campaign and its condition would continue to decline so long as it was forced to remain in the field through the awful autumn weather. The Association troops in particular had been on campaign almost continuously since May, in conditions that were already bad in the early summer. They had fought two major battles and various minor engagements. Now they were being expected to march and fight into the late autumn and winter. Montague records that on the 22nd and again on the 25th October the troops "*lay in the field all night*", while on the 9th November they were involved in skirmishes in the middle of the night. This must have taken a considerable toll on the health as well as the morale of the army. Increasing numbers of the troops were falling ill or deserting. There was nothing for the generals to do but retreat to the safety of their garrisons and prepare for a new campaigning season in 1645. Thus the Earl of Manchester returned eastwards, towards the Association. During the retreat, while at Aldermaston on the 17th November, Montague reports that they again expected the king would give them battle but did not.

Manchester therefore continued his march eastwards, to Reading and then to Aylesbury, to place the army in winter quarters.[159]

The Association army is said to have been hard hit at Marston Moor, being reduced from around 14,000 to about 6000 men, many of them sick or wounded.[160] However, according to Holmes, the losses in the battle were low. The same was true of the actions fought by Crawford's brigade during August, which had resulted in only a handful of casualties. This is confirmed by Davies' analysis of the changes in commanders during the year, which suggests that casualties were light throughout the army.[161] The one exception was the siege of York, where Crawford's brigade suffered badly in the disastrous assault on the Manor.[162]

The impact of the campaigns of 1644 on the army is reflected very clearly in Pickering's regiment. It was at its greatest strength, 738 men, in May 1644. After the siege of York and the battle at Marston Moor, it was reduced to 524, even though some recruits were still joining the regiment.[163] The reduction of the lesser garrisons during August was far less destructive, but sickness continued to take a toll. Hence in September, as the Newbury campaign began, Pickering's could muster only 362 men. By January 1645, after a further two months in the field, through the awful weather in October and November and without adequate supplies or pay, the regiment was reduced to just 243 men.[164]

Sickness had already been a problem as early as April 1644, for five sick soldiers from Pickering's own company had to be left at Cambridge when the army marched north.[165] At the Lincoln muster Axtell had six and Silverwood an unspecified number sick.[166] During the siege of York the army was decimated by an epidemic, possibly of typhus.[167] From Axtell's company alone at least 35 sick and wounded soldiers were left behind when the army returned south.[168] The actual numbers ill or injured must have been even greater, because some, perhaps less severe cases, were carried with the army as it marched south.[169]

There was still considerable illness during the autumn, because 61 men were recorded as sick at the St.Albans muster. Although they rejoined the regiment later, showing that sickness did not always lead to the men leaving the army, in early November more than 55 men had been sent home because they were ill.[170] Such losses are not surprising, for it is generally accepted that the common soldier was badly treated, suffering very poor living conditions and being poorly fed and clothed. He was not however left wholly without medical treatment. We find for example in July 1644 that Edward Webb, surgeon, was paid for curing two of Pickering's soldiers.[171] Illness was clearly a major reason for the decline in numbers in Pickering's, as in other regiments, but a significant cause was also desertion. There is frequent reference to men who had "*run away*".[172] Further losses through desertion during the winter were probably encouraged by the continued failure to pay the regiment. Indeed sickness and lack of pay, provisions and clothing, together with the abortive Newbury campaign, had demoralised the whole army.

The Eastern Association troops were quartered in several towns in Oxfordshire and Buckinghamshire during the winter of 1644-5. These garrisons, just beyond the borders of the Association, were facing the royalist capital at Oxford. While the army was in winter quarters, Major General Crawford retained control of some of the Association infantry, in Buckinghamshire. Pickering's however came under the overall command of Robert Browne, governor of Abingdon and Major General of Oxfordshire, Buckinghamshire and Berkshire.[173] Although he was a presbyterian, there is no indication of a direct conflict with Pickering. One wonders if the regiment had been placed with Browne because, as we shall see, Pickering would not accept Crawford's orders.

The regiment appears to have been quartered at Abingdon throughout the winter. Before the 15th of December 1644 we find

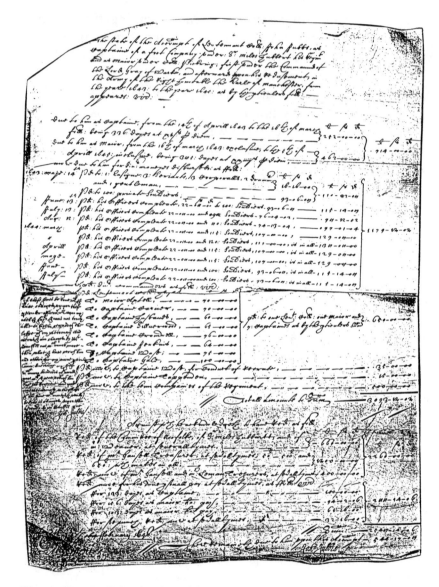

Figure 29 : Lt.Colonel John Jubbes' Account 1643-1646. An example of the detailed records which exist for Pickering's regiment. (Crown copyright)

"The State of the Accompt of Leutennant Coll John Jubbs, as Captaine of a foot Company under Sr Miles Hubbert his Regiment and as Maior under Coll Pickring, first under the Commaund of the Lord Gray of Warke, and afterward upon his Reducement, in the Army of the Right honourable the Earle of Manchester, from the yeare 1643 to the yeare 1645 as by the particulers full appeares vid:

Due to him as Captaine, from the 14th of Aprill 1643 to the 16th of March full: being 336 dayes at 15/- per diem £252-00-00, Due to him as Maior, from the 16th of March 1643 exclusive, to the 5th of Aprill 1645 inclusive, being 385 dayes at 24/- per diem £462-00-00   £714-00-00
moer due to him for diverse moneyes disbursed as ffull:

1643 Maye 14th Paid to 1 Ensign: 3 Seriants, 3 Corporalls, 2 drummers and 1 gent. £16-16-00
Paid to 100 private Souldiers £93-06-08   £110-02-09
June 13th Paid his Officers Compleate £22-0-80 to 100 Souldiers £93-06-9   £115-14-08
July 13 Paid his Officers Compleate £22-08-00 and 92 Souldiers £76-04-02   £98-12-02
Aug 12 Paid his Officers Compleate £22-08-00 and 80 Souldiers £73-13-04   £97-01-04
1644 march Paid his Officers Compleate £22-08-00 and 115 Souldiers £107-00-00 £129-08-00
march Paid his Officers Compleate £22-08-00 and 120 Souldiers £111-00-00is in all £138-08-00
Aprill Paid his Officers Compleate £22-08-00 and 115 Souldiers £107-00-00 is in all £129-08-00
maye Paid his Officers Compleate £22-08-00 and 115 Souldiers £107-00-00 is in all £129-08-00
June Paid his Officers Compleate £22-08-00 and 100 Souldiers £93-06-08   is in all £115-14-08
July Paid his Officers Compleate £22-08-00 and 100 Souldiers £93-06-08   is in all £115-14-08

If these somes be true which I have charged uppon these particuler officers (which upon my oath I sayd I was not truly able to saye in regard of the losse of my accompts) And whereas I am charged by Mr Gausell not with much more then what I have rec of him and others for my owne particuler Comp: but charge my selfe with many hundreds of pounds more which I received of him for the Regiment and payd owt accordingly to the Officers of the same which moneys I verily beleve is charged upon them already by Mr Gausell of me John Jubbes

moer, paid diverse Commaunders as full: vid: Paid Leutennant Col ......To Maior Axtell £70, To Captaine Carver £70, To Captaine Husbands £60, To Captaine Sillverwood £65, To Captaine Cromwell £76, To Captaine Jenkins £64, To Captaine Wase £75, To Captaine Gale £100
          paid to one Leut.Coll one Maior and 7 Captaines as by the particulers sum £650-00-00
Paid moer to Captaine Wase, for Conduct of Recrate £35, Paid to Captaine Tappenden £15, Paid moer to the ten Companies of the Regiment £500-00-00   Totall amounts to Sum £3093-12-02
Against which he acknowledgeth to have Recd as full: Recd of the Committee of Norfolke, of Sr Miles Hubbartt, and of Mr Weaver, at severall tymes £660-00-00, Recd of Mr Gausell Treasurer at severall tymes £50, £500 and £650 which makes in all   £1200-00-00
Recd of Mr Gausell and Mr Leman, Tresurers, at severall tymes £400-00-00   £2260-00-00
Recd moer for his owne personall pay at severall tymes, as ffull vid
ffor 133 dayes as Captaine £100-00-00, ffor 156 dayes as Maior half pay £94-02-06
ffor 103 dayes as maior half pay £61-16-00, ffor se...th Recd moer at severall tymes £32-16-00
                                                                              £299-14-06
Ja..ett ye 17th ffebruary 1646   Sum £2548-14-06
Coram Nobis   There Remaineth due to him upon this Accompt £544-17-08
Abra: Holditch
Job Throckmorton   John Jubbes "

Figure 30 : Richard Browne, Major General of Oxfordshire, Berkshire and Buckinghamshire. (Pryor Publications)

some of Pickering's men being moved from Sonning to Abingdon,[174] it was there on the 4th of January 1645 that the regiment was paid, and they were still there in April.[175] It is likely therefore that the regiment was involved in the defence of the town when Prince Rupert, with 1800 troops, attacked on the 10th January. New works had just been constructed around the garrison and these proved effective, for the royalists were driven back with heavy losses.[176] Pickering's were presumably involved in other minor actions while in winter quarters because, on the 5th of April 1645, Sir Samuel Luke wrote that two of Pickering's soldiers were among prisoners held by the royalists at Boarstall. This was one of the royalist outposts that ringed the king's capital at Oxford.[177]

In 1988-90 a Civil War cemetery was excavated at Abingdon, between St.Nicholas' Church and the Abbey. The cemetery contained some soldiers, in one case in a mass grave comprising nine individuals, as well as civilians. It is just possible therefore that some of those interred in the cemetery were from Pickering's regiment, or from the other Association regiments quartered in the town during the winter of 1644-5.[178]

Chapter 5

Into the New Model Army

Following the failures of 1644 there was a concerted effort to remove Manchester from command of the Association. Pickering was one of the officers who were questioned by parliament, in December 1644, about the events. Pickering reported the Earl's failure to capitalise on the successes of the early summer, his wish to winter in East Anglia rather than advance into the west, and his apparent unwillingness to defeat the king's forces.[179]

The conflict between Cromwell and Manchester had begun in early 1644.[180] Religion, as well as political views, played an important role in the dispute. In a *"Statement by an Opponent of Cromwell"* it is said that, like Cromwell, *"Colonels Montague, Russell, Pickering, and Rainsborough's regiments, (are) all of them professed Independents, entire."*[181] Both Manchester and Major General Crawford, his strongest supporter, were ardent presbyterians.[182] Pickering's and Montague's regiments are reported as, on Cromwell's instructions, absolutely refusing orders from Major-General Crawford during 1644.

The religious conflicts are reflected again in the various disparaging remarks made about Pickering's and Montague's regiments by Sir Samuel Luke, governor of Newport Pagnell, another presbyterian.[183] This dispute was part of the process that led to the eclipse of the Eastern Association army, which had proven to be the best organised and most successful of the parliamentarian forces. The conflict, between those who believed the war could be won and those who did not want to defeat the king, ultimately led to the success of the parliamentarian cause. It was the success of the Independents, like Pickering, which enabled the creation of an army committed to winning the war.

This New Model Army, which was established in April 1645, was placed under the command of Sir Thomas Fairfax. It is surely to Cromwell that we must look to see why Pickering's were put forward as a regiment for the new army. Pickering and his officers, as we have seen, had all the right credentials to fulfil Cromwell's objective of creating an effective army committed to complete military victory. When the list of officers for the New Model was debated in parliament Pickering, the "*fanatical Independent*", was, with Montague and others, struck out by the Lords. In fact, as perhaps the most radical regiment of all the parliament forces, Pickering's whole regiment was to be left out.[184] The opposition in the Lords was both on religious and political grounds, undoubtedly reinforced by Manchester's wish to purge his personal enemies from the New Model. However, following pressure from the Commons, Fairfax's original list of officers was eventually passed, by just one vote. Pickering's thus became the 12th regiment of the New Model Army.

Because the presbyterians failed in their dispute with the Independents over the remodelling of the army, Crawford refused to serve in the New Model Army. His regiment was placed under the command of Robert Hammond. Crawford transferred into Lesley's presbyterian Scottish army and he was sent to command at the siege of Hereford where he was killed, on 16th August 1645, by a musket ball as he viewed the fortifications. Crawford was buried in Gloucester Cathedral where, until recently, a monument existed to his memory.[185]

The new army comprised 12 regiments of foot, each with a nominal strength of 1200 men, 11 regiments of horse each of 600 men, and 10 companies of dragoons each of 100 men. Of these, three regiments of horse and four of foot came from Essex's army. Two regiments of foot were from Waller's army. The remaining nine regiments of horse and four of infantry came from the Eastern Association. The latter, comprising 3578 men, consisted of four regiments of foot, Crawford's, Rainsborough's, Montague's and Pickering's. Several other Association regiments were reduced into these and other New Model regiments.

Thomas Ayloffe was a presbyterian who had originally been included in the list of colonels for the New Model. During the winter of 1644-5, as the conflict between Independent and presbyterian was fought out, Ayloffe's were in the garrisons at Aylesbury and Newport Pagnell. There they were under the command of Crawford and Luke.[186] Ayloffe was not selected to serve in the New Model because of the failure of the Lords to purge it of 'radicals' like Pickering. It was therefore another 'Independent' regiment, Rainsborough's, which accompanied Pickering's and Montague's from the Eastern Association into the New Model Army.[187] However, as we have seen, there had been a drastic collapse in the numbers of men in Pickering's regiment during 1644 and early 1645. It was therefore decided by the Commons, on the 16th April, that Colonel Thomas Ayloffe's regiment should be reduced into Pickering's to help to bring the regiment up to strength. Ayloffe's, which probably drew its men from Essex,[188] had been raised under the same ordinance as Pickering's and Montague's. It had however spent most of 1644 and early 1645 in garrison at Aylesbury and Newport Pagnell. During that time they did not see action in any of the major battles, although they were involved in some minor engagements, such as the storming of Hillesden House.

This process of reorganisation was repeated throughout the parliamentarian army, because most regiments were under strength. So, for example, Rainsborough's were strengthened with troops from other Eastern Association regiments. Even those not transferring into the New Model were subject to similar reorganisation. So we find that Major General Browne's regiment was strengthened by the transfer of troops, as well as being given instruction to recruit new men. In Browne's case it was necessary to bring his regiment up to strength to make up for the loss from his command of the regiments transferring into the New Model. Ayloffe's had been with him throughout 1644 while Pickering's had supported him throughout the winter of 1644-5.

The soldiers from Ayloffe's were successfully transferred into Pickering's in early April.[189]

"To the honorable the Treasurer of the Army thees present Gentlemen
I might testify to youe that the offecers of Collo. Aliffs Regiment did with all willingness and request deliver unto us ther men according to order I shall intreat youe let the bearer heerof whome ther have sent Receive ther mony and as for my Rooles which I brought I shall desine that they may be auditted and the mony Redy and I shall waite one yoe this day to se in what forwardnes our recruts ar and dispach other busines for our Regiment and waite one youe tomorrow to receive the mony and shall ever rest

Your humble servant
Jo:Hewson [190]*"*

However, more recruits were still required. Though recruitment was probably still carried out in East Anglia, presumably now in Essex as well as Suffolk and Norfolk, it is likely that Pickering's acquired some men from other areas. The army as a whole was still seriously under strength and so in June Fairfax was empowered, for one month, to impress men in the areas through which the army marched.[191] Some 7000 men were conscripted into the New Model at this time. They could never have been adequately trained in time for the engagement at Naseby. The problems encountered by the foot, including Pickering's, during that battle may in part be explained by the presence in the ranks of many unwilling, raw recruits.

Pickering took with him into the New Model seven of his company commanders: Hewson, Jubbes, Axtell, Husbands, Jenkins, Carter and Silverwood.[192] Cromwell and Carver did not transfer with the rest of the regiment. It is possible that they were paid off, as some officers from other regiments had been, but they may equally well have transferred to more senior commands in other regiments.[193] In their place Gayle, formerly Captain Lieutenant in Pickering's own company, was made up to 6th Captain and Thomas Price, whose earlier history has not been traced, brought in as 7th Captain.[194] Not one Captain from Ayloffe's regiment was included, indeed it would appear that no commissioned officers transferred, for Hewson's letter clearly states that Ayloffe's officers "*delivered*" their men.[195] This was not simply a matter of political or religious differences. One objective of combining regiments was to redress the balance of officers to men. As can be seen from Appendix II, even when the numbers of common soldiers in Pickering's reduced to below 300 they retained a near full complement of officers.

Pickering took up his new command at Abingdon, where his regiment had been in winter quarters.[196] The Eastern Association ceased to be responsible for Pickering's regiment on the 5th of April 1645.[197] The total cost of maintaining the regiment over the previous ten months had been £4581/10/3d, of which £351/09/8d had been paid out for provisions and £51/01/2d for the pay of staff officers.[198] The administrative system of the Association had been unable to raise adequate resources to cover such large sums of money for so many regiments. This is why the pay to Pickering's regiment had fallen into arrears.[199] The situation regarding supplies and equipment for Pickering's and other Eastern Association regiments may however have been better than for some other Civil War armies. This is because the administrative organisation of the Association is considered to have been probably the most efficient of any that existed before the creation of the New Model Army.

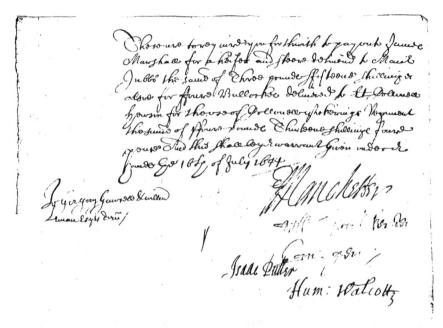

Figure 31 : An example of an Eastern Association warrant for payment for supplies. Payment for bullocks delivered for Pickering's regiment. (Crown copyright)

Pickering's were to find that the problems over pay did not improve, even after the transfer into the New Model. For 42 days in April and May 1645 the regiment was without any pay![200] This may have been a contributory factor leading to the mutiny in April 1645. This occurred when Colonel Pickering preached a sermon to his troops, following the confirmation of his command of the regiment.[201] However, it is perhaps to the men who had been transferred from Ayloffe's regiment that we should look for the cause of this trouble. They must have been influenced by the strong presbyterian views of their former commander. Many of Ayloffe's men had listed themselves as members of the Newport Pagnell garrison in April, presumably in an attempt to avoid transfer into Pickering's.[202] Most significantly, according to a royalist newsheet, it was Pickering's condemnation of presbyterianism to which the men particularly objected. That Pickering should have conducted lay preaching is not surprising, given his religious background. This was after all a significant element of evolving non-conformist practice, which continues today. That presbyterians should have reacted violently against it is equally understandable, for they wished to impose a new conformity in religion. Parliament, with its presbyterian majority, not surprisingly instructed Fairfax that preaching in the army was in future only to be conducted by authorised ministers.[203]

There was bad feeling between the regiments of the New Model and other regiments. In part this was because of the former's Independent religious and political views. It also however reflected resentment at the apparent rise in the status of the New Model regiments. These problems were exacerbated by the competition for resources. This is very clearly seen in the conflicts between the garrison of Newport Pagnell and Pickering's regiment, while the latter were in the south Midlands during May 1645. On the 19th of May Sir Samuel Luke wrote: "*There is such an antipathy here between my men and the New Model that you will every day hear of new encounters. My party which encountered Col.Pickering is returned with the loss of one man only, whom I intend to relieve so soon as I know where he is.*"[204] The general population may not however have shared the garrison's hostile views of Pickering. Luke later wrote that "*Col.Pickering exercises or exercises twice at North Crawley last Lord's Day, as I hear, and our townsmen at Newport admire him beyond Mr.Birdett.*"[205]

Chapter 6

The Campaign of 1645

On the 1st May Fairfax's army marched into the west, except for Cromwell with his party of horse and dragoons "*and four regiments of foot besides, who were ordered, when their recruits were come up, to joyn with him to busie the Enemy about Oxford.*"[206] It is likely that these were the four regiments of foot from the Eastern Association, with which Cromwell had worked so well during 1644. As we shall see, Pickering's were already with Cromwell in late April. Moreover, the brigade of infantry accompanying Cromwell was under the command of Major General Browne, under whose command Pickering's had remained throughout the winter. Rainsborough's, another of the former Eastern Association regiments, had also been placed under Browne's overall command in April and May 1645.[207]

Cromwell was already involved in an attempt to clear several smaller garrisons around Oxford. On the 25th of April, following a cavalry action, he had taken Bletchington House. Cromwell next turned his attention to Faringdon Castle, which was then in Berkshire but is now in Oxfordshire. This was a more difficult challenge and so he had to wait until the 29th of April for a body of infantry to join him before he could attack.[208] Five or six hundred foot were sent by Major General Browne from Abingdon. This was where Pickering's were quartered. The regiment was certainly present, because Sprigge reports that Captain Jenkins of Pickering's regiment was killed at Faringdon.[209] Pickering's may have numbered five or six hundred by this time, now that they had taken in the men from Ayloffe's regiment. It is therefore possible

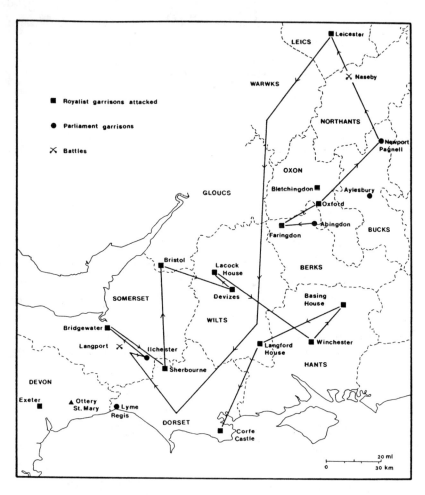

Figure 32 : The campaign of 1645.

that they were the only infantry regiment involved. The attack was abortive, for even with infantry Cromwell did not have the means for a decisive assault. Besides Captain Jenkins there were some fourteen men killed.[210] On the 3rd May Goring's horse and dragoons, from the south west, attempted to "*beat up*" Cromwell's quarters and to relieve Faringdon. They were engaged at Radcot Bridge by Cromwell's horse, who suffered some loss, but Goring did not press the action any further. It would not appear that the infantry was involved in the action.[211]

Having survived Cromwell's attack, the garrison at Faringdon remained in royalist hands until June 1646. However, nothing survives today of the Tudor mansion called Faringdon Castle. The house, which stood close to the church, has since been demolished and replaced by a late Georgian house.

On the 14th May Fairfax was recalled to besiege Oxford. Cromwell's and Browne's forces were also instructed to rejoin the army, which they did at Marston on the 22nd May.[212] Pickering was with the army at Southam in late May[213] and Hewson was involved in carrying arms and surgeons' equipment to the siege of Oxford.[214] It is however unclear whether the regiment was involved in any of the action against the lesser garrisons around Oxford.

Following the fall of Leicester to the royalist army on the 31st May, Cromwell was dispatched to secure Ely. Pickering's however remained with Fairfax. The army marched from Oxford on the 5th June, and by the 7th they were at Sherington, near Newport Pagnell. Pickering's appear to have been quartered at North Crawley, immediately north east of Newport.[215] The army was at Kislingbury by the 12th and then, following the king's army in its retreat from Daventry, at Guilsborough on the 13th. At Market Harborough that night the king decided to turn and engage the New Model.

The royalists marched south on the morning of the 14th June and the two armies met at Naseby. Pickering's were positioned at the centre of the parliamentarian front line, facing Bard's Tertio. On either side were the regiments of Sir Hardress Waller's and Edward Montague. For most of the rest of 1645 Pickering's would fight alongside these two regiments.

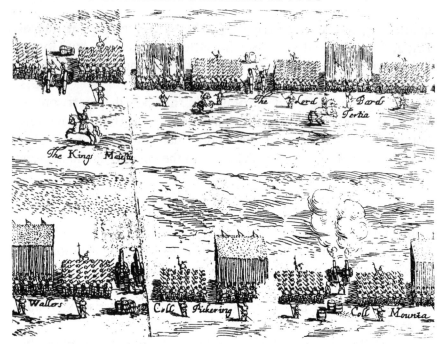

Figure 33 : Pickering's, Montague's and Hardress Waller's regiments on the front line at the battle of Naseby, from Streeter's engraving. (Northamptonshire Libraries and Information Service)

A royalist report of the battle records that *"..our forces advanced up the hill, the rebels only discharging five pieces at them, but over shot them, and so did their musquetiers. The foot on either side hardly saw each other until they were within Carabine Shot, and so only made one Volley; ours falling in with Sword and butt end of the Musquet did notable Execution; so much as I saw their Colours fall, and their foot in great Disorder..."*[216] After a short time the regiments in the parliamentarian front line broke. Sprigge recounts that *"The right hand of the foot, being the Generals Regiment, stood, not being much pressed upon: Almost all the rest of the main Battail being overpressed, gave ground and went off in some disorder, falling behinde the Reserves."*

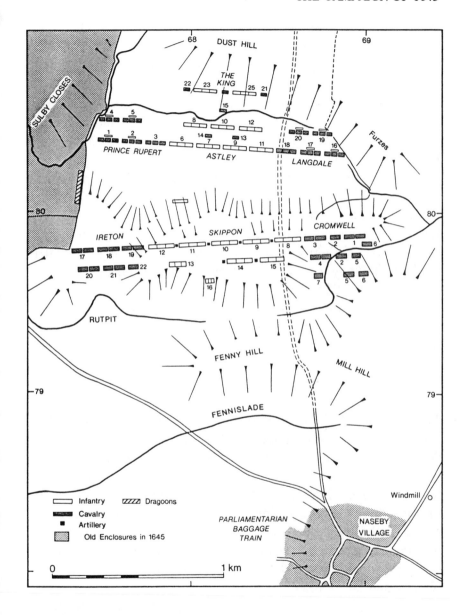

Figure 34 : Plan of the battle of Naseby, 1645

85

Pickering's regiment was one of these, for Baille, a presbyterian, wrote that "*the Independent Collonels Pickering and Montague flee lyke men.*"[217] Although the New Model Army had more infantry than the royalists, it is not clear whether in this initial assault the royalists were actually outnumbered. The royalists concentrated their attack against the infantry on parliament's left and centre. Of these regiments Pickering's, Montague's, Hardress Waller's and Pride's were, almost certainly, still seriously under strength. Only Skippon's is likely to have had anything near its full complement of men. Pickering's probably also had more than its fair share of raw recruits, for in January 1645 it had been the weakest of all the Eastern Association regiments, with only 243 men.[218] Moreover, although Ayloffe's troops had been taken into the regiment, it is unlikely that they were battle hardened. They had been a garrison force throughout 1644.

"*The Colonels and Officers, doing the duty of very gallant Men, in endeavouring to keep their men from disorder, and finding their attempts fruitless therein, fell into the Reserves with their Colours, choosing rather there to fight and die, then to quit the ground they stood on.*"[219] Pickering was undoubtedly one of those who chose to keep "*with the body, choosing rather to die, than leave the field.*"[220] The parliamentarian reserves moved forward and held the royalist advance. At the same time Cromwell, having dealt with Langdale's horse on the royalist left wing, turned his cavalry against the royalist infantry. While he attacked the royalist left flank, Okey's dragoons attacked their right flank. This gave the opportunity for the parliamentarian infantry regiments that had broken to be rallied and brought back into the action. So it was that Pickering's took part in the final destruction of the royalist infantry, which effectively decided the outcome of the battle of Naseby and hence the Civil War.

One of Pickering's captains, Tomkins, was killed, but there is no record of the losses amongst the enlisted men. Estimates at the time put the parliamentarian losses as a whole at between 50 and 100.[221] We can gain a better indication of the impact of the battle on Pickering's and other regiments from the numbers recorded as being seriously injured. Forty-nine men from Pickering's were listed, of which four later died of their wounds. The other regiments hard pressed in the front line were Montague's with 39, Hardress Waller's with 14 and Skippon's with 140 seriously injured. The remaining infantry regiments suffered far lower numbers of casualties.[222]

The following day, as the thousands of royalist prisoners were escorted towards London, the New Model marched north. They joined Cromwell's cavalry, who were already facing Leicester. On the 16th Fairfax summoned the town, but the royalist governor refused. The next day gun batteries were raised and a breach was created in the defences of the Newark, where the royalists had stormed the town two weeks before. Soon after the barrage began Lord Hastings, the royalist commander, proposed surrender. Pickering, this time with Rainsborough, was yet again appointed as commissioner to treat with the royalist garrison over the articles of surrender. The deliberations continued throughout the night, but early on the morning of the 18th the garrison marched out, leaving its weapons behind.[223]

Following a muster at Leicester, on the 18th June, the New Model advanced through Warwickshire, Gloucestershire and Wiltshire and was in Dorchester by the 3rd July. Lord Goring, commander of the royalist army of the south west, raised the siege of Taunton and took up a position at Langport to await the advancing parliamentarian army. The royalist garrison at Langport was in an important strategic position, controlling a bridge across the river Parrett. On the 6th July Fairfax sent Colonel Montague, with 2000 musketeers from three regiments, to the aid of Major General Massey, who was a short distance away near Ilchester. Massey was in command of several regiments of horse and dragoons, sent to follow and engage a large part of Goring's army which appeared to be marching once more on Taunton. The musketeers were sent to Massey because it was feared he would soon have to engage the enemy.[224] It is likely that the musketeers were drawn from Montague's, Hardress Waller's and Pickering's regiments, the brigade that fought together for much of 1645 and over which, for a brief period, Montague had command. Massey had however engaged and defeated the enemy before Montague arrived.

The next day, Thursday the 10th July, Goring drew up his remaining forces in a strong position a mile to the north east of Langport. The two armies were nearly equal in size, though Goring had sent his baggage and most of his artillery to Bridgwater. That morning the troops sent to assist Massey were recalled, but they did not rejoin Fairfax until the action was over. It is likely therefore that most of Pickering's regiment, having already missed the action near Ilchester also arrived too late to take any part in the battle of Langport. Because it was a landscape of hedged and ditched fields this was primarily a battle of musketeers and horse. It is therefore likely that Pickering's pike also had no significant part in the action.

A detachment of parliamentarian cavalry advanced along a hedged lane on the royalist position, which was defended by two cannon and by musketeers lining the hedgerows. Fairfax's horse were supported by musketeers. In the face of their advance the royalist army broke and ran. Goring's cavalry were pursued and attacked as they fled through the streets of Langport. His infantry regrouped for action but, without cavalry support, they had little option other than to surrender. The New Model had destroyed the royalists' last substantial field army.[225]

In contrast to what had happened with the Earl of Manchester's army following Marston Moor, Fairfax took every opportunity to capitalise upon his successes at Naseby and

Langport. A pattern was now established which would be followed throughout the rest of the year. Detachments of differing composition were sent to reduce lesser garrisons while the main body faced the major garrisons. Whereas Pickering's were involved in some of these lesser actions, for the moment they stayed with the main army. The next target was the small but strongly fortified garrison at Bridgwater.

The town was well supplied and manned, with 1800 troops under the command of Colonel Edmund Windham. The King had been led to believe that Bridgwater was "*a place impregnable*".[226] The town was divided in two by the river Parrett. The most heavily fortified part was on the west side of the river, which contained the Medieval castle with massive stone walls and a 30ft wide moat. The whole town was encompassed by a Medieval tidal ditch, which had been recut by the royalists. There were also stretches of surviving Medieval town wall, supplemented by new defences of earth and timber. Bridgwater is said to have had 40 guns mounted on its walls. Of these massive town and castle defences there is almost no trace remaining today. All that survives is a simple arch of the Water Gate to the castle, in the West Quay.[227]

The town was of strategic importance, controlling the lowest crossing of the river Parrett. Fairfax had to capture the garrison in order to consolidate his success at Langport. It was agreed that Bridgwater should be stormed rather than put to a protracted siege. Part of the New Model was on the west side of the river, while Pickering's were on the eastern side with Fairfax's, Skippon's, Montague's, Hardress Waller's, Pride's, Rainsborough's and Hammond's regiments.

On the 21st July "*About two of the clock in the morning, the storm began accordingly on this side of the town, (the Forces on the other side only alarming the Enemy...). Our Forlorn hope was manfully led on by Lt. Colonel Hewson; and as valiantly seconded by the General's Regiment ...... and the Major-General's .....*"[228] The ditch was crossed on portable bridges and the works scaled against strong resistance. Once inside, Pickering's opened the drawbridge for the other regiments to enter and soon that part of the town on the eastern side of the river was taken. *"There was not one officer of note slain, though many in person led on their men, and did gallantly, as Lt. Col. Jackson, Lt. Colonel to the General, and Col. Hewson of Col. Pickering's regiment."*[229]

Six hundred royalists still maintained the defences on the west side of the river. Having cut the bridge, the governor set fire to the eastern part of the town with a bombardment of red hot shot, leaving no more than three or four houses standing. On the 22nd the storming of the western part of the town was prepared by intensive cannon fire. In the face of this bombardment the governor soon surrendered, rather than allow the rest of the town to be devastated by fire as the eastern half had been. The parliamentarian troops were promised five shillings per man reward for the storming of the town. This was to be taken out of the sale of the goods captured in the siege. However, the troops still had not received anything by the 13th August. Indeed, it was reported that after Bridgwater various regiments, for want of pay, took free quarter and plunder quite unreasonably.[230]

Cromwell was now dispatched to deal with the Clubmen. These were local people who had taken up arms to protect their homes. They were supporting the royalists and causing the parliamentarian army considerable trouble. At the same time other forces were sent to besiege Bath, while Pickering was given the task of reducing another royalist garrison. On Sunday 27th July Fairfax *"sent a Brigade of horse and foot unto Sherborn under the command of that pious and deserving Commander, Colonel Pickering, to face the garrison, and to view the same; and if there were hopes to reduce it, to sit down before it, in order to a seige."*[231]

The garrison at Sherborne, under the command of Sir Lewis Dyve, was in the Medieval castle. They were proving particularly troublesome as they were encouraging the actions of the Clubmen against the parliamentarian forces. Colonel Pickering's brigade consisted of 2000 foot, supported by Colonel Whaley's Regiment of horse. On the 1st August Fairfax, with a few horse, came to Sherborne to view the works and castle. On the 2nd he ordered a "*close seige*", believing that it might be possible to quickly reduce the garrison.[232] Most of the army was brought up to Sherborne and they proceeded to constructed siegeworks around the castle. Dyve refused a second summons to surrender on the 6th August and so preparations were begun for an assault. Mines were dug and gun batteries were constructed. The twelve foot thick castle walls were unaffected by the army's artillery until demi-cannon arrived, by which time the siegeworks were within ten yards of the walls.[233]

On the 10th "*our great Guns began to batter the strong wall of the castle, between the two lesser Towers thereof, and had soone beaten down one of them, and before 6 of the clock that night, had made a breach in the wall, so as 12 abreast might enter.*" The castle, "*which the Enemy had vaunted would continue and hold out a half yeares seige at least, was most valiantly stormed.*"[234] Ingoldsby's men had gained the corner tower of the castle. Dyve then refused quarter and so the final assault was prepared. Under continued musket fire the defenders had to withdraw from the Great Court. Their position was becoming increasingly difficult and they were now running short of ammunition. By the 15th Dyve had no alternative but to surrender. In total 200 of the besieging force had been lost over the sixteen days. It is not known whether Pickering's suffered any casualties, for the exact role of the regiment in the attack is unclear.

The castle was plundered and later, in October, it was slighted. Despite this, large parts of the castle still stand today as an impressive ruin, in the care of English Heritage. Most of the new defences constructed at garrisons during the Civil War have been completely levelled over the last 350 years. However, at Sherborne the careful observed can pick out the earthwork traces of the triangular bastions and banks of the Civil War period, set immediately outside the Medieval castle ditch.

Although other minor garrisons were being cleared, Fairfax's main objective was now Bristol. Pickering's marched in the vanguard of the army, which assembled around Bristol on the 22nd and 23rd of August.[235] Sallies were made by the garrison over the following days against various regiments around the city. On the 29th the enemy attacked the parliamentarian quarters near Lawford's Gate. This was the area of the defences that Pickering's would attack on the 10th of September, but they may not have been involved in these skirmishes. It appears that they only moved into this position on the 9th.

It was decided that the city should be stormed, because Fairfax was not confident that his army could maintain a long siege. By the time of the assault on Bristol the command of the General's Brigade, comprising Fairfax's, Montague's, Pickering's and Sir Hardress Waller's regiments, had fallen to Colonel Montague.[236] They were to attack on both sides of Lawford's Gate, while other brigades attacked on the north and the west sides of the city. Montague's and Rainsborough's Brigades crossed the Avon at Kensham to Stapleton where they quartered that night. Montague's Brigade then secured the area between the rivers Froom and Avon, coming up to within musket-shot of Lawford's Gate.[237] On the morning of the 10th a concerted attack was mounted. A new earthwork defence, with forts set along it, had been constructed outside the Medieval town walls.[238] To cross these fortifications the soldiers carried faggots to fill in the ditch while some brought up ladders to scale the ramparts. Pryors Hill Fort, on the north side of the Froom, was captured but to the south

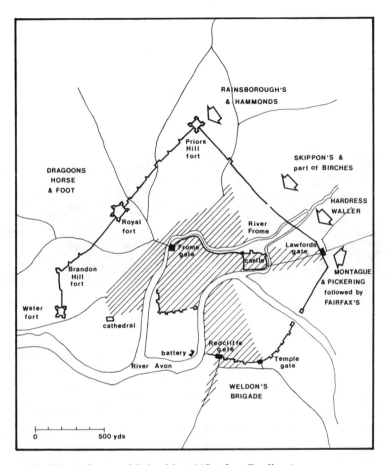

Figure 35 : The defences of Bristol in 1645 (after Gardiner)

of the Avon the attack failed against the much more substantial defences. The decisive assault took place on the eastern side of the city. It was here that Montague's Brigade stormed the defences *"on both sides of Lawford's Gate, bothe to the river Avon, and the lesser river Froome."* Pickering himself *"entered gallantly, and with others gave the royal party that wound, which will hardly ever be healed."*[239]

93

Figure 36 : A view of Bristol in the 18th century from the Brandon Hill, site of one of the Civil War forts. Pickering's attacked the most distant suburb towards the left.

Cromwell wrote that "*Col. Montague and Col. Pickering, who stormed at Lawford's Gate, where was a double work, well filled with men and cannons, presently entered; and with great resolution beat the Enemy from their works, and posessed their cannon. Their expedition was such that they forced the Enemy from their advantages, without any considerable loss to themselves. They laid down the bridges for the horse to enter;.... Then our foot advanced to the Castle Street: whereinto were put a Hundred men; who made it good.*"[240] Prince Rupert now requested a parley and once again Pickering, with Montague and Rainsborough, was responsible for the negotiations with the royalists.[241] The garrison surrendered on the following day.

In all during the action Pickering's and Montague's captured 22 great guns and took many prisoners.[242] For such a hazardous assault on one of the major towns in the kingdom the

94

losses were remarkably light. It was reported that in *"Col. Rainsboroughs and Col Montague's Brigade, not fortie men are lost"*,[243] while in total the parliamentarian army suffered no more than 200 killed. Pickering's may not have suffered many casualties but Captain Gayle, formerly Captain Lieutenant in Pickering's own company, was killed during the attack.[244]

Today, apart from the earthwork remains of the fort on Brandon Hill, which now lie within a public park, nothing survives of the defences of Bristol. Of Lawford's Gate only the street name remains to show where the decisive action was fought in 1645.

Montague was now called to London and so command of the brigade, which had fought together since Naseby, changed once more.[245] Such transfers of command seem to have followed according to seniority, as with company command. Montague had taken up his commission first, in 1643, Pickering in 1644, while Hardress Waller took command of his regiment in 1645. Hence Pickering took over from Montague and, following Pickering's death, Sir Hardress Waller came to command the brigade.[246] However, it is clear that the brigade was not a fixed unit. Its composition could change according to the circumstances. Sometimes the brigade would have additional regiments assigned to it, at other times it might be under more senior command.

Following the fall of Bristol the army was again divided and the clearance of the lesser royalist garrisons continued. Rainsborough was sent with a brigade to take Berkeley Castle, while Cromwell took another brigade, comprising Montague's, Pickering's, Hardress Waller's and Hammond's, to take Devizes and Laicock House.[247]

Devizes town and castle had been fortified to command the county of Wiltshire and control traffic from London to the West. The governor was Sir Charles Lloyd with a garrison of 300 or 400 men. On the 17th September the town was quickly overrun forcing the garrison to retreat to the castle. Though much of the site was in ruins, the gatehouse was intact. Cromwell summoned the castle but was denied. Artillery was therefore brought up from Trowbridge and a battery of ten guns set up in the market place, within pistol shot of the castle. The bombardment by both cannon and mortars began on the Monday and played on the castle all day and night. One mortar shell even fell within the old roofless keep, which was being used as a magazine, though it did not explode. This bombardment quickly convinced the governor to discuss terms and on the 23rd September the garrison surrendered.[248] Today all that survives of the fortifications of Devizes are the earthworks of the Medieval castle. The buildings have long since gone, replaced by a 19th century castellated mansion. The only remaining evidence for the siege now lies in St.John's church, where later repairs still reveal the scars caused by cannon balls during the bombardment.[249]

Pickering was now given command of a brigade, comprising his own and two other regiments, and dispatched to take Laicock House. This garrison lay about seven miles north west of Devizes on the Chippenham road. It had been held at various times by either side, though the owners, the Talbots, were royalists. In the summer of 1645 Laicock was held for the king. The governor, Colonel Bovile, "*considering, that neither Bristol nor the Devizes were able to hold out against our force, did easily resolve, that a Poore house was much lesse able; (though in truth there were good works about it) accordingly therefore upon the first Summons, he came to conditions of surrender...*"[250] The garrison marched out on the 26th September.

Today Laicock still survives as a pleasant country house owned by the National Trust. Though it has seen some later alterations, it retains much of the character of the 17th century mansion. However there are no significant remains of the Civil War fortifications in the parkland or gardens. They have presumably been obscured by later landscaping.[251]

Figure 37 : The Medieval West Gate of Winchester, viewed from inside the city, earlier this century. The castle lay immediately to the left.

By the 28th September the brigade had rejoined Cromwell, who now advanced to Winchester.[252] The city, which still retained most of its Medieval defences, was well fortified. The garrison was based in the castle, which before the war had been acquired as a home by Sir William Waller. According to Hugh Peters, who walked around the site after the surrender, the castle was heavily defended, with "*six distinct works and a drawerbridge....it was doubtless a very strong piece, very well victualled.*"[253] It was said to have been "*as strong a place as any in England.*" Estimates of the strength of the garrison vary between 500 and 700.[254]

On the 29th, in the face of unexpected resistance, the city was entered after the firing of a bridge or gate.[255] The governor, William Ogle, then retreated with his troops into the castle. Cromwell wrote of the events: "*I am come to Winchester on the*

97

Lord's day... with Colonel Pickering, commanding his own, Colonel Montague's, and Sir Hardress Waller's regiments. After some dispute with the Governor, we entred the Town; I summoned the Castle, was denied, whereupon we fell to prepare our Batteries...."[256] Within four days the gun batteries were ready. Soon after the barrage began a second summons was refused. The next day there was a continual bombardment, with some 200 shots being fired. This created a stormable breach, near *"a Black Tower"*, wide enough for the entry of 30 men abreast. However, Pickering's and the other infantry regiments did not have to take the castle by storm. During the night the royalist soldiers began to desert and the officers demanded a parley. As a result, on the 5th October, Ogle surrendered.[257]

Figure 38 : The Great Hall of Winchester Castle, with a fragment of the castle wall, in 1787.

98

A report of the events at Winchester records: "*It may be easily conceived that such an active army needs be a great spender of men by sickness or otherwise, though blessed be God it appears at every siege the enemy's swords cut not off many. At this of Winchester, I know not above two or three soldiers lost.*" Indeed, Cromwell probably gained far more troops than he lost, for some of the royalist soldiers enlisted with the New Model Army after the surrender.[258]

Although two of the gates and fragmentary remains of the city walls still stand at Winchester, there is almost nothing to see of the castle. It was slighted after the war. Today only the 13th century Castle Hall remains, one of the finest Medieval halls in England. It lies next to the West Gate of the city and is now used as a law court.

It was mistakenly reported at this time that, from Winchester, Cromwell had sent Pickering to reduce Longford House. In fact all of Cromwell's troops now moved on to Basing House. This was a royalist garrison that had proved a major problem for the parliamentarians throughout the war. "*Basing Castle, the seat and mansion of the Marquisse of Winchester, stands on a rising ground, having its forme circular, encompassed with a brick rampart lyned with earth, and a very deep trench, but dry. The loftie Gate-house with foure turrets looking northwards, on the right whereof without the compasse of the ditch, a goodly building containing two faire courts, before them is the Graunge, severed by a wall and common roade...*"[259] Basing House today is no more than a fragmentary ruin in the care of Hampshire County Council. However, visitors to the site can appreciate the scale of the fortifications which existed in the 17th century from the massive earthworks that still survive. Short stretches of the wall and a single turret of the far weaker outer defensive circuit still stand to almost their original height. In places they retain the crude musket loops from which the defenders could fire on the besieging

Figure 39 : The surviving gate through the outer brick built defences of Basing House.

troops. The outer gate is also partially intact, with the arms of the Paulet family displayed above. Outside the defences the large barn or grange, which provided cover for some of the attacking troops, also still stands. Thanks to the extensive excavations of the site early this century there is archaeological as well as documentary evidence for the 17th century castle and of the sieges of 1644 and 1645.[260]

Until Fairfax arrived the house had stood invincible. " *They that have seen and viewed it say that it was a peice made as strong and defensible as nature and art could imagine.* "[261]

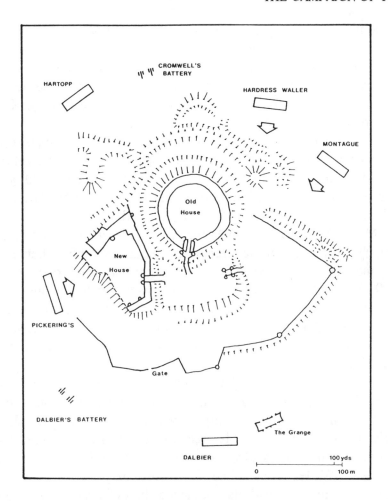

Figure 40 : Plan of Basing House siege, 1645.

Several earlier sieges, both blockades and frontal assaults, had failed to reduce this royalist stronghold. An alternative strategy was therefore decided upon, the employment of scientific siege engineering. Colonel Dalbier had begun the siege on the 20th of August and, having very carefully prepared his positions, started

101

his bombardment in late September. Soon a major collapse in the structure began. Cromwell arrived with the heaviest of the siege pieces on the 8th October. Forts and sconces were then raised by the besiegers completely enclosing the garrison. When the heavy cannon opened fire from newly dug positions on the 12th October two great breaches were made.

Dalbier had already prepared siegeworks, which had approached almost to the foot of the royalist defences. Therefore at 5.00 or 6.00am on Tuesday the 14th the assault began. Colonel Dalbier was on the north side of the House next to the Grange, Pickering's were to his left, then Hartop's, Sir Hardress Waller's and Montague's. The royalists immediately abandoned the outer defences. Estimates of the strength of the garrison range between 300 and 800, compared with a parliamentarian force of perhaps 7000. The defenders must simply have been too few to man the extensive outer defences against such a massive attacking force. They retreated into the two houses, the massive Medieval shell keep called the Old House and the later mansion known as the New House.

Dalbier's artillery had been directed against the New House. The cannon fire had created a massive breach in the walls, which can be seen in a contemporary engraving (figure 41). It is likely that it was through this breach that Pickering's entered the House, once they had scaled the outworks. While Montague's and Hardress Waller's assaulted the strongest works, where Cromwell's artillery had also breached the defences, Pickering's stormed the New House. They had soon passed through the New House and into the bailey that separated it from the Old House. *"They in the Old House hung out some black ensigns of defiance, and set a fire on a bridge over which our men were to pass, disputing the passage at swords point, and the rest in the house threw out granadoes amongst our men, whereby many of them were killed."*[262]

Figure 41 : A view of the New House at Basing, by John Dunstal circa 1652, showing the breaches through which Pickering's probably stormed the House (Ashmolean Museum, Oxford).

Once Pickering's had taken the gatehouse to the Old House the defenders *"summoned a perley, which our men would not hear."*[263] It is not surprising to find Pickering taking a valiant part in this attack, because Basing was well known as a papist garrison. For many of his men however, it may have been the thought of the great wealth of this mansion that encouraged them in the assault.

103

The artillery bombardment continued as the attack on the Old House proceeded. Within three quarters of an hour, at about 7.30am, all resistance was broken.[264]

The parliamentarian losses were estimated at the time between ten and forty, with royalist losses of between 100 and 300. Amongst those taken prisoner were Inigo Jones, the famous architect, Hollar, the engraver, and the Marquis of Winchester himself. During the rest of the day the soldiers proceeded to plunder the mansion, the wealth of which "*was of greater value than any single garrison could bc imagined.*" They must have considered this a just reward for the day's action. Moreover, as we have seen, the New Model troops had not received regular pay during the previous year. Accidentally during this plundering the House was set on fire and destroyed. What had not been destroyed by the fire was then demolished to stop Basing ever being used again as a royalist garrison.

It had been reported on the 9th October that "*This day we understand the valiant little Colonel Pickering is set down before Langford House, belonging to the Earl of Coleraine, within four miles of Salisbury.*" This must have been incorrect for, as we have seen, Pickering's were at Basing House. They did clear the Longford garrison, but only after Basing had fallen.[265] Longford Castle, as it is now known, was a fortified house built in the 1590s. It held a garrison of about 100 men.[266] Hewson and Major Kelsey were sent to treat with the governor, Lieutenant General Pell. In the face of superior forces, and with no hope of relief, the garrison surrendered without a shot being fired.[267] The house was not slighted but it was later deserted and by the 18th century it was ruinous. However, today it is again occupied, having been sympathetically restored in the 19th century.[268]

Almost the only substantial garrison now left between London and Exeter was at Corfe Castle. By the 20th October, at the request of the Western Association, Fairfax had sent troops to

Figure 42 : Longford Castle in the early 19th century.

assist in the siege of Corfe. Initially it was just Pickering's regiment that joined Colonel Bingham, the governor of Poole, to lay siege to the castle.[269] This massive Medieval castle lay in a strong defensive position and very well fortified. It could not be reduced as easily as so many other garrisons had been in 1645. The besieging force set up gun batteries facing the castle. The earthworks of a Medieval siege castle, which can still be seen a quarter of a mile to the south west of Corfe castle, were reused for one of the parliamentarian gun batteries. This was to be a long siege. Corfe did not surrender, nor did it succumb to a quick assault. This was because it was not in a key strategic position and so did not warrant the artillery or troops necessary for a major assault. These forces were instead concentrated around Exeter, a far more significant royalist garrison. However, on December the

105

Figure 43 : An artist's impression of the siege of Corfe Castle, Dorset.

16th, Fairfax did send further troops to Corfe, comprising one regiment of horse and two regiments of foot. These included Rainsborough's, for we know that on the 25th December they were sent on from Corfe to Oxfordshire to support the Abingdon garrison.[270] It is not clear whether Pickering's were present throughout the siege, but the castle did not finally fall to Bingham until early March 1646.[271]

Corfe was comprehensively slighted by the parliamentarian forces after the siege so that it could never again be used by the royalists. However the destruction was not total. Today Corfe castle, which is owned by the National Trust and open to the public, remains one of the most spectacular of all our ruined castles.

Figure 44 : Corfe Castle as it was in the early 19th century. The towers are ruined and tumbling into the ditch, just as they were left by the parliamentarian forces who slighted the castle.

Chapter 7

The Death of Colonel Pickering

During the winter of 1645-6 the New Model Army lay before Exeter. The soldiers were quartered in villages around the city, while the army headquarters were at Ottery St.Mary, a small market town ten miles east of Exeter. Though his regiment was at the siege of Corfe castle, by the 12th November John Pickering was at Ottery St. Mary. Once more, for the last time, we find Pickering involved in discussions with the representatives of a royalist garrison. Together with Ireton and the Judge-Advocate he was attempting to negotiate the surrender of the city of Exeter.[272]

During the Civil War there were probably more soldiers who died of disease than died on the battlefield. The winter of 1645-6 at the siege of Exeter was no exception. Plague had been rife in and around Bristol at the time of its capture, in September, but the parliamentarian forces had apparently escaped its effects. However, by early November the New Model Army was beset by a new disease that was claiming many lives. Presumably the plague had been brought from Bristol, but had taken a month or more to take hold in the army. It is thought that this disease was influenza.

The foot "*were sick in most places, there dying of Souldiers and Inhabitants in the Town of Autree [Ottery St.Mary], 7, 8, and 9, a day, for severall weeks together, insomuch that it was not held safe for the headquarter to be continued there any longer.*" Many soldiers probably succumbed easily to illness because they were so poorly supplied. As Hugh Peters had reported from the army in October, "*It is most certain that of 21 weeks the horse are 12 weeks behind, and the foot have likewise their proportion of sorrow through want of pay. I know three score in one company lying sick by eating of raw roots and green apples through want of money to buy proper food.*"[273] The officers lived in far greater comfort and had a much better diet, so one may expect they had greater resistance to illnesses. They were not however immune to the diseases that camp life encouraged. So it was that Pickering himself fell ill while at the army headquarters in Ottery St.Mary. Like so many of the common soldiers he did not recover. On Monday the 24th of November 1645, just before his 30th birthday, *"Col.Pickering, that pious, active Gentleman, that lived so much to God, and his Country, and divers other Officers, dyed of the New disease in that place; Six of the generals own family were sick of it at one time, and throughout the foot regiments half the Souldiers...."*[274]

The victims of the 'plague' were apparently not recorded in the parish register, and there is a dubious claim that they were buried in a communal grave in Bury Meadow.[275] However, Pickering was given a funeral and a burial place appropriate to his rank. It must have taken some time for the news to reach Pickering's family and so the arrangements for the funeral were not made until more than two weeks after John had died.

On the 10th of December 1645 Cromwell wrote from Tiverton to Colonel Ceely:

"Its the desier of Sir Gilbert Pickeringe, that his deceased Brother, Col. Pickeringe should bee interred in your guarrison; and to the end his funeral may bee solemnized with as much honour as his memorie calls for, you are desired to give all possible assistance therein; the particulars will be offered to you by his Major, Major Gubbs, with whome I desier you to concurr herein, and believe itt, Sir, you will not only lay a huge obligation upon myselfe and all the Officers of this armie, but I dare assure you the General

himself will take it for an especial favor, and will not lett it goe without a full acknowledgement. But what neede I prompt him to soe honourable an action, whose owne ingenuitye wil be argument sufficient heerin. Whereof rests assured your humble servant,

Oliver Cromwell" [276]

In 1644 and 1645 Colonel Ceely was governor of Lyme Regis in Dorset. This was the nearest parliamentarian garrison to Ottery St.Mary. It lay just 15 miles to the east and had remained staunchly parliamentarian throughout the war.[277] Unfortunately the burial register for 1645-6 does not survive for the town, nor is there any record of a monument to John in the parish church. It is therefore impossible to prove beyond doubt that Pickering was buried at Lyme. The only other likely place for John's interment was Ottery St.Mary itself and, though the burial register for 1645 survives, there is no reference to John Pickering.[278] It is quite unthinkable, given his national standing, the influential position of his brother and the wishes of Cromwell and Fairfax, that John could have been given an unrecorded burial like a common soldier. There can be little doubt therefore that Sir Gilbert's wishes were carried out, and that John Pickering was buried at Lyme Regis in mid December 1645.

The high esteem in which Pickering was held by many parliamentarians can be seen in the various reports of his death in the newsheets of the time. The article in the Moderate Intelligencer was accompanied by an elegy. Sadly it is far less eloquent than his cousin John Dryden, later to become poet laureate, might have produced, but he was only fourteen at the time.[279]

"Now that Bethel [280] and he are gone; For reward, garlands, or crowns for all their faithfull services, and valiant sections for their country, let England mourn them, lest the War outlive the

Worthies; And it shall melt us into teares, to think, that these should not live to see the fruit of their service and share in the benefit upon earth. but the will of the lord be done. " [281]

Another newsheet records:

"The Souldiers are overwhelmed with grief, deare, gallant, Pickering is dead, the Champions, nor Oracles can cease to mourne since glorious Pickering is gone; the heaviest blow that England received this winter... "

"England, thy Commons and thy Peeres,
Out from their eyes gush brinish teares;
Black Autumn fruits to cinders turne;
Birds cease to sing, our joy is fled,
'Cause glorious Pickering is dead,
Let Time contract the Earth and Skie,
To recommend thy memorie
To future ages, to rehearse
Thy worth in drerie sacred verse,
Whilst we unto the shades repaire,
Where trees do eccho sighing aire;
Or to some melancholly cave,
In whose dark entrailes is a grave
Where shrouded we may mourne at night
For Britaines losse of such a light. " [282]

Pickering's standing in the army cannot be overestimated, for Sprigge devotes a whole page to a poem on his death:

"But whosoever would have me proceed in my story, must give me leave first to weep a while this sorrowfull verse, over deer Colonel Pickerings Hearse.

111

IOHANNES PICKERING
IN GOD I RECKON HAPINES
Vain all our profer'd Ransoms are,
There's no discharge in the Graves war:
Well They may shew; yet they cannot,[283]
What a brave Captive death hath got.
Only, t'amuse our discontent,
(For Passion kils, that has no vent:)
Might thy wisht presence find excuse,
(Of whom we made too little use)
Wee'ld ask (swift Poster) whose great haste[284]
Was ne'r before the Kingdoms waste:)
Why posts thou from's? Because we rest,[285]
which suited not thy active brest
Did that Antiperistasis
Fire thy fine Spirits to thy blisse?
Must thou be scaling Heaven alone,
For want of other action?
Would thou hadst took that leisure=time,
To visit some responsal=Clime.
Or, must hard Censures, (voyd of love)[286]
Be expiate by thy remove?
Or, Covetous, couldst thou not stay
For wages, till the end o'th' day?
Or could no vantage mend thy stature,[287]
(To see our triumphs) under Nature?[288]
But 'tis in vain to ravel more,
W'have nothing but thy Name t'adore:
That Oracle gives the best guesse,
Wherein we heare thee thus professe,
IN God I RECKON HAPINES. "[289]

John Pickering did not inherit much land or property and so did not leave a substantial estate. He never married and so left no children. What he did bequeath was a regiment that would have a significant impact in the events that followed during the next decade. The success of Pickering's regiment, later known as Hewson's, including the advancement of its senior officers, was a clear reflection of the success of the Independents.

The character of John Pickering's regiment did not arise by chance. It was surely created around John's own character and beliefs. As Commissary General for the Musters in 1643 and early 1644, and as an associate of Cromwell, he was in the ideal position to establish a regiment that mirrored his own religious and political views. It was, after all, not just John, but his whole regiment that drew extreme criticism from the presbyterians. Of all the regiments nominated for the New Model Army, it was Pickering's alone which the Lords wished to be struck out *en bloc.*

It was surely John's deep religious conviction, in the eyes of his enemies his fanatical Independency, that was his strength in the Civil War. Such beliefs gave him and his colleagues a courage, certainty of purpose and deep commitment to succeed that was essential in winning such a war. In the context of peace such strengths could, and in many of his associates did, become a disasterous weakness.

John Pickering's close colleagues, Montague and Hardress Waller, saw great advancement under Cromwell. Edward Montague became a Councillor of State and then Admiral of the fleet. Sir Hardress Waller became a Major General. Though one or two of John's senior officers may have been drawn down a path that they later regretted, John Hewson and Daniel Axtell, like John Pickering's brother Gilbert, were also willing partners in the actions of the Commonwealth and Interregnum. They were close to the centre of power throughout, as allies and supporters of Cromwell, right through to the extreme of military dictatorship.

There can be little doubt that had John lived he would, like his family, friends and military colleagues, have played a significant role throughout the Interregnum.

Colonel John Pickering was typical of the men behind the Cromwellian revolution, while his regiment was one of those that provided the military power base which enabled Cromwell to achieve that revolution, for better or for worse.

Chapter 8

Postscript : Colonel Hewson's Regiment

After Pickering's death, command of the regiment fell to his Lieutenant Colonel.[290] Hewson was well prepared for the new responsibilities. At various times he had already taken command while Pickering was elsewhere on army business. The other officers were similarly promoted according to seniority.

Pickering's had been a radical regiment from the start, but it became an increasingly authoritarian force as the revolution itself moved towards military dictatorship. Conflict with the king had thrown together various puritan sects and political factions in a common cause. However, as the war progressed the differences between the presbyterians and the more radical groups developed into open conflict. In this the regiment was firmly on the side of the radicals, pressing to win the war by military means and championing the cause of religious freedom. John Pickering literally practiced what he preached. The events in the regiment in the spring of 1645, with the mutiny that John's lay preaching provoked, was a microcosm of the conflict between presbyterian and Independent within the parliamentarian cause.

Following the end of the first Civil War, the bonds between the various radical groups became increasingly strained, as a radical army challenged a presbyterian parliament. The Levellers and Independents may have been close in their religious beliefs, but differences in ideas over the social order became increasingly apparent during 1647 as the political debate progressed. Hewson's regiment experienced that political conflict within its own ranks. This is clearly seen in a comparison between the attitudes and actions of the senior officers. In 1647, as in 1645, the course which the regiment took the revolution itself was to follow.

In May 1647 the presbyterian parliament attempted to break the military power base of the Independents. They required the New Model Army regiments to disband or to volunteer for the Irish campaign. Hewson's regiment refused, as did others. It was Lieutenant Colonel Jubbes, together with Major Axtell and two other 'agitators', who prepared a statement of the grievances of the regiment.[291] In June, as political debate intensified in the army, some in Hewson's regiment were clearly committed to the political agenda of the Levellers. Of the six authors of 'A Letter from the Army to all the honest Seamen of England' dated the 21st June 1647, two were from Hewson's regiment. They were Captains Alexander Brayfield and John Carter. A third, Azariah Husbands, had been a Captain in the regiment. In addition Edmund Garne and Daniel Hincksman, also from the regiment, were amongst the 17 ordinary soldiers from 9 regiments who also signed the letter.[292]

Jubbes, in his statement in the Putney debates, on the 1st November 1647, called for political reforms extending well beyond mere army grievances. His position was a conciliatory one between Independent and Leveller, seeking even to bring the liberal presbyterians into an agreement. In some respects he wanted the sort of settlement which finally came with the Glorious Revolution of 1688. For Jubbes the war had encouraged pacifist views. He came to see a real conflict between, in his own words, the "slavery of the sword" and Christian peace. In April 1648, having lost the debate within the regiment, as the Levellers did within the army as a whole, and as a second Civil War approached, Jubbes laid down his sword and took up the pen.[293] He was disillusioned with the course the revolution was taking, believing that Cromwell was diverting the cause of liberation.[294]

Opposed to the war in Ireland and saddened by the suppression of the Levellers, Jubbes pressed for political change from outside the army. He became associated with a group of London radicals more moderate than the Levellers. Social radicalism was at this time linked to millenarian ideas. It is not therefore surprising to find that Jubbes was one of the believers in the Second Coming of Christ, confidently looking forward to the personal reign of Jesus on earth.[295]

In attitude and ideas Hewson differed markedly from Jubbes. On the 22nd February 1648, following a soldier petition to Fairfax, Hewson expressed a typically authoritarian view about the Levellers: "*We have had tryal enough of Civil Courts, we can hang 20. before they will hang one*".[296] His views were close to those of Cromwell, who later remarked angrily about the Levellers, "*you have no other way to deal with these men but to break them or they will break you...*"[297]

Jubbes was replaced as Lieutenant Colonel by Daniel Axtell,[298] while John Carter became Major. The concerns that they had expressed in 1647 about liberty apparently no longer bothered them. Under Hewson, Axtell and Carter, the regiment would go on to become an important tool of suppression. It was involved, with Sir Hardress Waller's, in Pride's Purge, the action of the army against parliament, and remained obedient when some other regiments supported the Levellers.

In 1648, during the second Civil War, Hewson's faced the Kentish royalists. Hewson himself was commended for his valour and resolution when the regiment bore the brunt of the fighting at the storming of Maidstone. Fairfax wrote: "*I cannot but take notice of the valour and resolution of Col. Hewson, whose Regiment had the hardest task (Major Carter, his major, being hurt and Captaine Price, a deserving and faithfull Officer, slain).*"[299] Hewson and Axtell were voted £100 and £150 respectively by parliament in recognition of this service. With Rich's regiment, they suppressed the rising in Kent and recaptured the castles at Deal, Walmer and Sandown.

Figure 45 : John Hewson. An engraving by Van der Gucht. (By courtesy of the National Portrait Gallery, London)

In December the regiment was part of the force with which Fairfax occupied London, and its commanders remained close to political events as they unfolded. Hewson was a judge at the trial of the king, also signing the death warrant, while Axtell commanded the guard at the king's execution. In April 1649 Hewson's were chosen, by lot, to go to Ireland with three existing and six new regiments. While in Ireland they took part in many of the major actions and the most notorious, particularly the siege of Drogheda, as Cromwell ruthlessly took control of the country.

Hewson had not received a university education before the war, but in 1649 he was given an MA by Oxford University. He commanded the regiment in Ireland and later became governor of Dublin, member of the Council of State and Member of Parliament. Though knighted by Cromwell and described as "*an arch-radical and religious zealot*", he did not approve of Cromwell's "*usurpation*". He opposed Cromwell from within the Protectorate, at some risk to himself.[300] In October 1656 Hewson took active military command once more. His regiment was made up of companies of the Irish army which had been sent back in early 1655 when a royalist rising was anticipated.

Throughout the Protectorate Hewson maintained a position of political influence, while his military standing was recognised in 1658 with his admission to the Honourable Artillery Company.[301] To the very end, his regiment was at the heart of the action. As the collapse of the military dictatorship came closer, on 19th August 1659 they were involved in the suppression of Booth's Rising and on the 5th December in controlling the London riots.

In 1660, with the restoration of the Long Parliament, the command of Hewson's regiment was given to a former quartermaster-general, John Streeter. The many changes through which the regiment had passed are perhaps best exemplified by the fact that troops from Pickering's old regiment took part in the last action of the Commonwealth.

Figure 46 : Daniel Axtell. (By courtesy of the National Portrait Gallery, London).

We find the regiment fighting against its original first Captain, Daniel Axtell. Axtell had thrown in his lot with Lambert, in one last desperate attempt to reimpose the military government of the Major Generals. On Sunday 22nd April Ingoldsby's regiment, with Captain Linley's troop of Rossiter's and two companies of Streeter's, encountered Lambert's forces near Daventry in Northamptonshire, and routed them.[302] Though Axtell escaped, he was later captured and eventually executed as a regicide.

At the Restoration Hewson fled to the continent where he died in about 1662, probably in Amsterdam. In July 1660 his former regiment was placed under the command of the cavalier Lord Bellasis and in October it was disbanded. However, four of its companies were retained to form the garrison at Hull.[303] So, in one sense, the regiment which had first served under Colonel John Pickering in April 1644, survived longer than any other of the parliamentarian regiments created during the Civil War.

Appendix I

Colonel Montague's Journal, 1644

A summary of Montague's record of the march of the Eastern Association army during 1644[304] For maps see figures 14 & 24.

KEY TO MAPS	DATE	MONTAGUE'S QUARTERS (HEAD QUARTERS)
1	1st February	To Newport Pagnell, Bucks - lay there 11 weeks "and whilst wee layd there wee tooke Hillseden house Sr Alexander Daynton..."
2	20th April	To Goldington, Beds.
3	21st	Buckden and Brampton
4	22nd	Barnwell (Oundle)
5	23rd	Collyweston & Duddington (Stamford)
6	29th	Buckeminster & Sewston (Gosforth?)
7	30th	(Grantham)
8	2nd May	Wellingore & Navenby (Navenby)
9	3rd	Lincoln - "were wee tooke the City the same day the Enemye running up the hill or Closse which wee tooke also the 6th day. 50 officers and between 700 or 800 prisoners and about 60 slayne with all theire greate Guns Carriages Arms and Ammunucion."
10	8th	Torksey
11	13th	Gainsborough
12	20th	Belton in Isle of Axholme
13	21st	Thorne
14	23rd	Doncaster
15	25th	Thorne
16	27th	Wistow (Selby)
17	1st June	Osbaldwicke (Heslington)
18	3rd	Clifton - York siege
19	16th	Stormed the Manor House, York
20	1st July	Raised the siege
21	2nd	Marston Moor - "wee fought and roughted theire Armye tooke 20 greate Peices 12000 small armes all theire carriages 1700 prisoners and slayne 1150."
22	3rd	kept the field
23	4th	Bishopthorpe
24	6th	Heslington - siege of York
25	16th	city yielded

26	20th	Kyrkeby Wharfe (Tadcaster)
27	22nd	(Sir John Ramsden's House near Ferrybridge)
28	23rd	Wheatly Sandon & Barneby upon Don (Doncaster) -"whilst there Tickhill Castle and Welbecke House were yielded unto us upon Composition."
29	1st August	Rotherham - Crawford's, Montague's and Pickering's regiments detached from main army
30	2nd	Sheffield - yielded 10th
31	13th	Bolsover castle - yielded 14th
32	17th	Little Normanton, Thorneton [?Morton] & Pilsley
33	18th	Allferton
34	21st	Wingfield Manor [S.Wingfield] - yielded
35	23rd	Mansfield
36	24th	Redford
37	25th	Gainsborough
38	2nd September	Nettleham
39	3rd	Ashby - rejoin main army (Digbye)
40	4th	Osbournby (Sleaford)
41	5th	(Bourne)
42	6th	(Paston)
43	7th	Farcet in Northants
44	9th	Wyton & Houghton (Huntingdon)
45	10th	near Gamlingay
46	11th	Baldock (Bigglesworth)
47	12th	Winly [Wymondley?] (Hitchin)
48	13th	(St.Albans)
49	14th	Conge [?Colney]
50	21st	Bushey (Watford)
51	23rd	Denham (Uxbridge)
52	26th	White Walton (Maidenhead)
53	27th	Wargrave (Reading)
54	29th	Ruscombe & Hurst
55	5th October	Willington, Hants - Montague's and Hubbard's regiments
56	6th	Newbury
57	17th	West Sherborne
58	19th	Basingstoke then West Sherborne
59	20th	Basingstoke
60	21st	Hackewood Parke
61	22nd	through Basingstoke to Mortimer - met the Lord General's army and the City brigades. Lay in the field all night.
62	23rd	Reading
63	24th	Bucklebury
64	25th	Thatcham - "were wee lay in the ffeild all night".
65	26th	To the field near Shaw by Newbury
66	27th	"Wee fought with the kings Armye lyeinge in Shaw and Newbery and Dinnington Castle, and drove then out of the Townes were

123

		wee tooke 356 Prisoners with the Earle of Cleveland and the Lady Rutham 7 ffield Pieces the kinge flyeinge towards Bath wth 10 men only".
67	2nd November	From Shaw to Compton
68	3th	East Hagborne in the vale of the White horse
69	6th	Buckleberye
70	7th	Speene & Marsh Benham - "were we had 12 great shott made against us from Dinnington Castle they espeying our Colours"
71	9th	Newbury - "at 12 o'Clocke in the night at which tyme the Kings Army releived Dinnington Castle were we had some skyrmishes with them tooke some Prisoners and made theire wholl Bodye to retreate towards Wallingford."
72	10th	"We Marche into the feild after them, and same day backe to Newberye".
73	17th	Aldermaston - "were wee expected the kinge would have given us battle but they did not soe much as face use with a Partye."
74	18th	Mortemore
75	19th	Paternoster Hatch in Heckfield
76	20th	Reading
77	22th	Riscombe & Wargrave
78	26th	Maidenhead
79	3rd December	Ammersham
80	4th	Wendover
81	5th	Aylesbury - outside the workes in Waltham
82	9th	Wendover
83	10th	High Wycombe
84	11th	Henly on Thames

Appendix II

Composition of the Regiment
April 1644 - February 1645

		APRIL	8 MAY	23 JUL	15 FEB
COLONEL	John Pickering	1	1	1	1
CAPTAIN LIEUTENANT	Reynold Gale[1]	1	1	1	1
ENSIGN	John Mowsier[2]	1	1	1	1
SERGEANT	Samuel Bailey[3]	3	2	3	2
CORPORAL		3	3	3	3
DRUM MAJOR		1	1	1	0
DRUMMER		1	1	1	0
G. AT ARMS		2	2	2	1
CLERK		0	1	1	1
G. OF COMP.		0	6	6	2
TOTAL OFFICERS		13	19	20	12
SOLDIERS		81	51	36	29

Reference is also made to a reformado Lieutenant Hammond.[4]

---

[1]   PRO SP 28/25 f.6; /267 ff.89 & 91; /128 f.138.
[2]   PRO SP 28/128 f.118; /24 f.512.
[3]   PRO SP 28/24 f.536; /128 f.138.
[4]   PRO SP 28/25 f.9, Aug. 1644.

COLONEL JOHN PICKERING'S REGIMENT OF FOOT

		APRIL	8 MAY	23JULY	15 FEB
LT.COLONEL	John Hewson	1	1	1	1
LIEUTENANT	John Toppenden[1]	1	1	1	1
ENSIGN		1	1	1	1
SERGEANT		2	3	3	3
CORPORAL		3	2	2	3
DRUMMER		2	2	2	1
G. AT ARMS		2	2	1	1
CLERK		0	1	1	0
G. OF COMP.		0	4	4	6
TOTAL OFFICERS		12	17	16	17
SOLDIERS		80 - 106	49	53	25

GENERAL STAFF OF THE REGIMENT (listed under the Colonel's Company except the apparent second Quartermaster and Provost Marshall, listed under Hewson's Company in July) :

WAGONER	Nich. Pickering?[2]	1	1	1	0
Q.MASTER	John Dausen[3]	1	1	2	1
PR.MARSHALL	John Ewen[4]	1	1	2	0
SURGEON		1	1	1	1
SURG.'S MATE	John Cliffe[5]	1	1	1	0

---

[1]   PRO SP 28/25 f.21; /267 f.89.
[2]   PRO SP 28/25 f.207.
[3]   Possibly Dancer. PRO SP 28/25 f.210; /128 f.118; /267 f.91.
[4]   PRO SP 28/25 f.211.
[5]   PRO SP 28/25 f.208.

		APRIL 1644	8 MAY 1644	23JULY 1644	15 FEB 1645
MAJOR	John Jubbes	1	1	1	1
LIEUTENANT	David Dolly[1]	1	1	1	1
ENSIGN	Smyth[2]	1	1	1	1
SERGEANT		2	2	2	2
CORPORAL		3	3	3	3
DRUMMER		2	1	1	0
GENTLEMAN AT ARMS		0	1	1	1
CLERK		0	1	1	1
GENTLEMAN OF THE COMPANY		2	4	2	3
TOTAL OFFICERS		12	15	13	13
SOLDIERS		98	66	67	35

SURGEON		0	0	1	0

---

[1]   PRO SP 28/25 ff.32-3; /267 f.88.
[2]   PRO SP 28/25 ff.32-3.

COLONEL JOHN PICKERING'S REGIMENT OF FOOT

		APRIL	8 MAY	23JULY	15 FEB
CAPTAIN	Daniel Axtell	1	1	1	1
LIEUTENANT	Peter Dawkyns[1]	1	1	1	1
ENSIGN	Wm.Bagly[2]	1	1	1	1
SERGEANT		2	2	2	2
CORPORAL	Henry Sparrow[3]	3	3	3	2
DRUMMER		2	2	2	1
G. AT ARMS		2	1	1	1
CLERK		0	1	1	1
G. OF COMP.		0	1	1	3
OFFICER TOT.		12	14	14	13
SOLDIERS		81	52	38	29

AXTELL'S ACCOUNT for April 1644 - April 1645 (dated 29th February 1646) :

	Ap 4	Ap 15	Jul 12	Jul 26	Sep 18	Oct 15	No 26	Jan 4	Feb 15	Ap 12
Sergeant	2	2	2	2	2	2	2	2	2	2
Corporal	3	3	3	3	3	3	3	3	3	3
Drummer	2	2	2	2	2	2	2	2	2	2
Gent. at Arms	1	1	1	1	1	1	1	1	1	1
Soldiers	100	93	80	62	38	41	41	34	34	34

---

[1]   PRO SP 28/25 f.43.
[2]   PRO SP 28/25 f.43.
[3]   PRO SP 28/243 unfol., receipt 24th Oct.1644.

		APRIL 1644	8 MAY 1644	23JULY 1644	15 FEB 1645
CAPTAIN	Azariah Husbands[1]	1	1	1	1
LIEUTENANT		1	1	1	1
ENSIGN	John Daynes[2]	0	1	1	1
SERGEANT		1	2	1	2
CORPORAL	Elmoore[3] Ganes	3	1	1	2
DRUMMER		0	1	0	0
GENTLEMAN AT ARMS		0	1	1	1
CLERK		0	1	1	1
GENTLEMAN OF THE COMPANY		0	2	2	2
TOTAL OFFICERS		9	10	9	11
SOLDIERS		75 incr. to 100	42	24	27

[1]   PRO SP 28/267 f.88.
[2]   PRO SP 28/25 f.56.
[3]   PRO SP 28/26 pt.1 f.60.

129

COLONEL JOHN PICKERING'S REGIMENT OF FOOT

		APRIL 1644	8 MAY 1644	23JULY 1644	15 FEB 1645
CAPTAIN	John Jenkins	1	1	1	1
LIEUTENANT	Mark Davy?[1]	1	1	1	1
ENSIGN		1	1	1	1
SERGEANT		2	2	2	2
CORPORAL		0	2	3	2
DRUMMER		0	2	2	0
GENTLEMAN AT ARMS		0	1	1	2
CLERK		1	1	1	1
GENTLEMAN OF THE COMPANY		0	2	3	2
TOTAL OFFICERS		6	13	15	12
SOLDIERS		3 incr. to 34	46	27	25

---

[1]   Possibly Marke Danil. PRO SP 28/25f.65; /267 f.88.

		APRIL 1644	8 MAY 1644	23JULY 1644	15 FEB 1645
CAPTAIN	Cromwell	1	1	1	1
LIEUTENANT	Edward Lunn[1]	1	1	1	1
ENSIGN		1	1	1	1
SERGEANT	Thos. Barfoot?[2] Humfrey Everet[3]	2	2	2	2
CORPORAL		3	2	3	3
DRUMMER		1	1	1	0
GENTLEMAN AT ARMS	Thos.Chapman[4]	1	1	1	1
CLERK		0	1	1	0
GENTLEMAN OF THE COMPANY		0	0	1	0
TOTAL OFFICERS		10	10	12	9
SOLDIERS		12 incr. to 37	50	22	12

---

[1]   PRO SP 28/267 f.88.
[2]   PRO SP 28/25 f.75.
[3]   PRO SP 28/128 f.126.
[4]   PRO SP 28/25 f.75.

COLONEL JOHN PICKERING'S REGIMENT OF FOOT

		APRIL 1644	8 MAY 1644	23JULY 1644	15 FEB 1645
CAPTAIN	Carver	1	1	1	1
LIEUTENANT		1	1	1	1
ENSIGN	Rayner[1]	1	1	1	1
SERGEANT		1	2	1	2
CORPORAL		3	3	2	2
DRUMMER		1	1	1	0
GENTLEMAN AT ARMS		0	1	1	1
CLERK		0	0	1	0
GENTLEMAN OF THE COMPANY		2	1	2	2
TOTAL OFFICERS		10	11	11	10
SOLDIERS		77	60	28	18

---

[1]   PRO SP 28/25 f.91.

		APRIL 1644	8 MAY 1644	23JULY 1644	15 FEB 1645
CAPTAIN	Ware then John Carter	1	1	1	1
LIEUTENANT	Farrant?[1]	1	1	1	1
ENSIGN	Barcock[2]	1	1	1	1
SERGEANT		2	2	2	2
CORPORAL		3	3	3	2
DRUMMER		1	1	2	0
GENTLEMAN AT ARMS		0	1	1	1
CLERK		0	1	1	0
GENTLEMAN OF THE COMPANY		0	2	2	1
TOTAL OFFICERS		9	13	14	15
SOLDIERS		90 incr. to 100	50	30	16

---

[1] PRO SP 28/25 f.80.
[2] PRO SP 28/25 f.82.

		APRIL	8 MAY	23JULY	15 FEB
CAPTAIN	John Silverwood	1	1	1	1
LIEUTENANT	Gwyne[1]	1	1	1	1
ENSIGN		1	1	1	1
SERGEANT		2	2	1	1
CORPORAL		3	2	2	3
DRUMMER		2	2	2	2
G. AT ARMS		0	1	1	0
CLERK		0	1	1	1
G. OF COMP.		2	2	2	2
TOTAL OFFICERS		12	13	12	12
SOLDIERS		91	57	34	27

Silverwood's Account (dated 1646) : Silverwood claims to have paid 100 soldiers in April 1644.

SOURCES

APRIL, MAY, JULY 1644 :
PRO SP 28/25; Pickering's Company - ff.1-3; Hewson's Company - ff.15-18; Jubbes' Company - ff.27-29; Axtell's Company - ff.34, 36, 38; Husband's Company - ff.49-51; Jenkins' Company - ff.57-60; Cromwell's Company - ff.68-70; Carver's Company - ff.76-78; Ware's Company - f. 83; Carter's Company - ff.94-5; Silverwood's Company - ff.195-7.

FEBRUARY 1645 : PRO SP 28/26 f.308

AXTELL'S ACCOUNT APRIL 1644 - APRIL 1645 : PRO SP 28/276 unfol.
SILVERWOOD'S ACCOUNT : PRO SP 28/267 f.133.

---

[1]   PRO SP 28/25 f.202.

Notes

1. Presumably Wynanderwath, now Winderwath near Brougham. A.H.Smith, 1967, *'Placenames of Westmorland'*, vol.II. For a more comprehensive account of the whole Pickering family in the 16th and 17th centuries see J.Anderson Winn, 1987, *'John Dryden and His World'*, Appendix A. Other relevant articles, though including some significant errors, are P.D.Mundy, *'The (Dormant) Baronetcy of Pickering of Titchmarsh'*, in *'Notes and Queries'*, June 1953, p.250-3; and *'The Pickerings of Aldwincle All Saints, Northamptonshire'* in *'Notes and Queries'*, November 1952, p.490-2. There are miscellaneous notes on the family pedigree in the Dryden Mundy Collection, NRO. I have been unable to trace Bryan L'Anson, *'The Records of the Pickering Family'*, referred to by Mundy.

2. Lay Subsidy 1525AD.

3. J.Goring and J.Wake, 1975, *'Northants Lieutenancy Papers 1580-1614'*, Northamptonshire Record Society, vol.27.

4. D.Brunton & D.H. Pennington, 1954, *'Members of the Long Parliament'*, p.69-71.

5. The Pickering family portraits were apparently sold at Christies in the mid 1920s. They are said to have included a portrait of one of Gilbert and Elizabeth's sons. A.M.W. Stirling, 1924, *'Life's Little Day'* (Thornton Butterworth). I have also been unable to trace any likeness of John Pickering or of his brother Gilbert. The portrait of Gilbert's wife, Elizabeth, is reproduced by Helen Belgion, 1979, *'Titchmarsh Past and Present'*.

6. Shadwell's poem, *'The Medal of John Bayes'*.

7. DNB. According to Noble, 1787, *'Memoirs of the Protectoral House of Cromwell'*, vol.1, p.379-380, Gilbert's second wife was a daughter of John Pepys of Cottenham, Cambridgeshire. This was Samuel Pepys' family, with which the Pickerings were friends. Noble must be wrong as Elizabeth outlived Gilbert by 11 years. Noble is incorrect in various other matters, for example mistakenly attributing John's military actions to Gilbert.

8. Northamptonshire Record Society pamphlet 1290.

9. VCH, *'A History of the County of Northampton'*, 1970, vol.2, p.136.

10. The most damning assessment of Gilbert derives primarily from the papers of Jeremiah Stevens, Rector of Quinton and Wootton, Northants. He was one of Gilbert's victims, being sequestered in 1644. J.Walker, 1714, *'Sufferings of the Clergy'*, p.91. H.Isham Longden, 1942, *'Northamptonshire and Rutland Clergy'*, vol.XIII, p.55.

11. J.Bridges, 1791, *'History & Antiquities of Northamptonshire'*, vol.2, p.381.

12. Letter in NRO, Baker Manuscript 12069.

13. RCHM, 1975, *'An Inventory of the archaeological sites in Northamptonshire'*, vol.1, p.100, site 25, suggests that the manor is the building north west of the church in 1779. This conflicts with the information in Belgion, op.cit.n.1, p.64. The issue has not been adequately resolved.

14. Hearth Tax 1662, NRO Microfilm 25.

15. Belgion, op.cit.n.1.

16. G.Markham, 1625 *'The Souldiers Accidence'*, p.31. *'The Visitation of Northamptonshire, 1681'*.

17. NRO, Titchmarsh Parish Registers.

18. John Milton, *'The Second Defence'*, quoted by D.Wolfe, 1944, *'Leveller Manifestoes of the puritan Revolution'*, p.2.

19. Oundle School Register. Gilbert Pickering may also have attended the school, but the register only begins in 1626, by which time he was at university.

20. NRO, ML116, 1565AD.

21. W.G.Walker, 1956, '*A History of Oundle Schools*', plate 8 & p.92. Plans and elevations of the building in 1850, showing it substantially as it was built in 1485, are given by Walker, p.76-7.

22. R.Flower, 1989, '*Oundle School and the English Public School*', p.39; DNB; Walker, op.cit.n.21.

23. Unfortunately St.Catherine's College Admission Register, which begins in 1627, is not comprehensive. It took at least a year to matriculate, hence John was probably admitted in 1629 or 1630.

24. Visitation, op.cit.n.16, p.171; J. & J.A. Venn, 1924, '*Alumni Cantabrigienses*', vol.3, p.359.

25. Gilbert Pickering, Clare College, 1570; Henry Pickering, Christ's College, 1582; Lewis Pickering, Emmanuel College, 1587. Venn, op.cit.n.24.

26. W.H.S. Jones, 1936, '*A History of St.Catherine's College*', p.92-3.

27. Audit List, St.Catherine's College archive.

28. S.Smith, '*Fellow Commoners and the College Plate, 1473-1875*', in E.Rich, ed, 1973, '*St.Catherine's College Quincentenary Essays*'. Book of matriculations and degrees....1544-1659, St.Catherine's College archive.

29. RCHM, 1959, '*City of Cambridge*', vol.II, p.182.

30. '*The Moderate Intelligencer*', 28th November 1645.

31. DNB.

32. D.Brunton and D.H.Pennington, 1954, '*Members of the Long Parliament*', p.6.

33. NRO, YZ1311; YZ1315, 1638AD, copy of the will of John Pickering Esq. of Grayes Inne, Middlesex.

34. Op.cit.n.33.

35. N.Pevsner, 1952, '*The Buildings of England : London*', p.212-4.

36. '*Commons Journals*', ii, 315 and 330. Sprigge p.156.

37. HMC, '*Mss of the Duke of Buccleuch & Queensbury*', vol.1, p.301.

38. PRO, SP28/128 part 1, money disbursed by the Cambridge Committee, 25th October 1642, £2 to John Pickering.

39. HMC, 1932, '*Mss of the Duke of Hamilton*', vol.21, p.61-68, letters from John Pickering; '*Calendar of State Papers Domestic 1641-43*', p.446, Feb.28th 1643, warrant of the Committee for Safety of the Kingdom to Sir Gilbert Gerard, Treasurer of the Army, to pay £180 to John Pickering, employed by both Houses into Scotland, for his expenses, in addition to £100 already paid; p. 6 Nov. 1643, receipt of Edward Pickering for £100 for John Pickering regarding his work in the North.

40. Winn, op.cit.n.1, p.33. Several verses, of little poetic merit, by John Pickering addressed to his friend Whiting in the preface to Nathaniel Whiting's poem of 1637, '*Le Hore du recreatione*'. It is not proven beyond doubt that this is not our John Pickering, for Nathaniel was an eccentric Cambridge wit who became a puritan divine, and after the restoration he acted as Congregationalist minister to Lady Pickering. He was at Cambridge at the same time as John. J.R.S. Whiting, '*A 17th Century Northamptonshire Poet Parson*', in '*Northamptonshire Past & Present*', vol.4, p.223-232.

41. VCH, op.cit.n.9, vol.3, p.14.

42. BL, Egerton 2651, f.163, pay for John Pickering as Commissary in the Eastern Counties, 1643.

43. H.Hexham, 1642, '*The Principles of the Art Militarie*', part 2, p.4.

44. HMC, 7th Report, '*Mss of G.A.Loundes*', 696.

45. HMC, op.cit.n.44, 705, 22 August; 720, 25th August.

46. PRO, SP28/128, part 8, payment to Commisary [Pickerell] for his pay till the 1 Jan last (1644) £56/10/0; SP 28/14 f.114, 26 March, paid Commissary Pickering his pay till Jan 1st (1644) £56/10/0.

47. PRO, SP28/25, part 3, f.471, payment to Col.Pickering as Commissary General for 16 days between 25th March and 20th April 1644.

48. HMC, op.cit.n.44, p.698.

49. A.Kingston, 1897, *'East Anglia and the Great Civil War'*, p.137-8; J.Rushworth, 1682, *'Historical Collections'*, vol.5, p.283; op.cit.n.30.

50. Kingston, op.cit.n.49, p.137-8. However, Colonel Russell was referred to by Cromwell as Mr.Russell, p.28 above.

51. Op.cit.n.30.

52. Kingston, op.cit.n.49, p.151; *'Lords Journals'*, vi, p.415. PRO, SP28/143, f.17, however shows on 20th Feb (1644) he was still making payments as Comissary Pickering.

53. PRO, SP28/24 f.519 & /128 f.118. Payments at Bury on 28th Jan.& 2nd Feb.; £240 to Pickering from the Suffolk Committee. This might imply recruitment of his dragoons from Suffolk.

54. Op.cit.n.30; *'Mercurius Aulicus'*; *'Mercurius Civicus'*, March 7th 1643-4; H.G.Tibbutt (Ed.), 1963, *'The Letter Books of Sir Samuel Luke'*, 4th March 1643, to Earl of Essex; F.W.Bull, 1900, *'A History of Newport Pagnell'*, p.155-168; *'Weekly Accompt'* 20-28 Dec.1643, *"..whiles the forces in the Associated Counties are now raising"*.

55. F.P.Verney, 1892, *'Memoirs of the Verney Family during the Civil War'*, p.192-3.

56. T.Carlyle, (Ed.), 1858, *'Cromwell's Letters and Speeches'*, p.146.

57. F.R.Harris, 1912, *'The Life of Edward Montague'*, p.29; J.J.Shehan, 1862, *'History and Topography of Buckinghamshire'*.

58. Verney, op.cit.n.55, p.193.

59. Op.cit.n.30.

60. *'Mercurius Aulicus'*, 9th March 1643/4, p.866-8.

61. Rev.H.Roundell, 1863, *'The Garrison of Newport Pagnell'*, in *'Records of Buckinghamshire'*, vol.2, p.232-3. Tanner Papers, 1643, vol.2, f.591.

62. Verney, op.cit.n.55, p.195.

63. PRO, SP28/25 f.52-95.

64. Op.cit.n.30.

65. G.Davies, 1931, *'The Army of the Eastern Association'*, in *'English Historical Review'*, vol.46, p.88-96. The Association forces comprised five regiments of horse: Manchester's, Cromwell's, Vermuyden's, Fleetwood's and Sir John Norwich's; three regiments of dragoons: Lilburne's, Ayloffe's and Walton's; and seven regiments of foot: Manchester's, Huggin's, Hobart's, Russell's, Montague's, Crawford's and Pickering's. Davies omits Ayloffe's regiment of foot or incorrectly identifies it as a dragoon regiment. For some reason Pickering was still apparently being paid as Commissary General up to the 20th of April 1644.

66. PRO, SP28/25 ff.52-95, 195-211 and 471. In early April we find £300 being paid by the Association to Col.Pickering *"to provide necessaries for the Regiment his owne"*, SP28/14 f.114 & f.150. The accounts of all the companies start during March or April, and in the case of Captain Carver it is specifically stated that the start of his account is from *"the day of the date of his Commission"*, SP28/25 f.76.

67. PRO, SP28/267, f.91, during March or April arms for the regiment were being repaired in Cambridge.

68. C.Holmes, 1974, *'The Eastern Association'*, p.145.

69. PRO, SP28/24 f.536, 18th July 1644, Mr.Leeman "*to paie unto Sam Bailey Corporall under Capt Gales, of Colonell Pickering's regiment one weeke paie to advance him to the Army*".
70. *'The Kingdomes Weekly Intelligencer'*, Saturday October 11th 1645.
71. G.Foard, forthcoming, *'The Ensign during the English Civil Wars'*.
72. Markham, op.cit.n.?.
73. The claim that Pickering's and Montague's regiments had blue coats and Hardress Waller's black coats originates from G.N.Godwin, 1904, *' The Civil War in Hampshire (1642-5) and the story of Basing House'*. Godwin misinterpreted the report in the Kingdomes Weekly Intelligencer, op.cit.n.70. The error is repeated in J.Adair, 1981, *'They saw it happen: Contemporary Accounts of the Siege of Basing House'*, p.71, n.1.
74. HMC, op.cit.n.44, f.738, 2nd September 1643, Committee of the Association to Sir Thomas Barrington of the Essex Committee, "*...we have provided red coats for such as we have sent away of yours, we shall trust to you to furnish the rest, and to send the arms, drums, colours, and other accoutrements*".
75. Carlyle, op.cit.n.56, vol.1, p.380.
76. *'Calender of State Papers Domestic 1644-5'*, p.358.
77. 500 Red Coats at 10/- per coat for Col. Russell's regiment, PRO, SP28/24 f.388; Bill to Mr.Harlockenden for Essex for 341 coats: Item to Lt.Col.Cliffon 141 Red Coates £77/10/0, SP28/25 f.345; Account of money due to Thomas Bucher, SP28/26, pt.I, f.136. The green coats faced red could be Manchester's own regiment according to Young, 1973, *' The English Civil War Armies'*.
78. Mr.Moody's bill for 5240 coats, PRO, SP28/128 f.10; Order to Samuel Moody for 1000 coats "*at the usual rate*" for the Lynn garrison, £475, SP28/19 f.257; 10 coats for the Lord General's lifeguard £5/10/0, SP28/24 f.281, 1644; op.cit.n.77.
79. January 1645: "*3 buff coates at 30/- the peece being in all £4/0/0*", PRO, SP28/35 f.640.
80. C.H.Firth, 1967, *'Cromwell's Army'*, p.238-8.
81. "*Item the 13th April 1644 to Daniel Axtell for your Regiment 1000 shirts as your warrant and aquittance on the file for shirts appeareth which comes to .....*", PRO, SP28/128 f.118.
82. Musket repairs: 19 April 1644 : bill of Willerton the Smith for repair of muskets of Silverwood's company, PRO, SP28/25 f.415; warrant for payment £1/2/4, SP28/128 f.136; Bill for the repair of muskets for Captain Wase's company, SP 28/25 f.416; warrant for the payment of £1/9/11 to Robert Chumbe for fixing arms for Captain Karver, 1 May 1644, SP28/128 f.128. "*Paid for fixing the Regiment's Arms in Cambridge £2/1/0*", 4 or 26 April 1644, SP28/267 f.91.
83. PRO, SP28/24 f.191.
84. PRO, SP28/25 f.415.
85. Kingston, op.cit.n.49, p.190.
86. PRO, SP28/25 f.312, payments 14th February 1645; SP28/26, pt.1, f.331, payments 14th October - 9th December 1644; SP28/257 unfol., Account of Lt. Col. John Jubbes 1643 - 1645, payments to Jubbes by John Cory of Norwich, high collector for the weekly assessments.
87. PRO, SP28/243 unfol., Receipt of Henry Sparrow 24th Oct. 1644. Order for payment to Humphrey Everard 4th Oct. 1644; SP28/519, an account of money laid out by the Committee at Bury, January 28th, £90, February 2nd, £150.
88. *'Calendar of State Papers Domestic 1644-5'*, p.387.
89. Davies, 1931, p.95; Temple 1985, *The Original Officer List of the New Model Army'*, in *'Historical Institute Journal'*; Sprigge.

90. A.Wood (Ed. Bliss), '*Fasti Oxonienses*', quoted by J.Foster, 1891, '*Alumni Oxonienses 1500-1714*'.

91. Holmes, op.cit.n.68, p.176; Davies, op.cit.n.65.

92. Schenk suggests Jubbes may have been the brother of William Jubbes of Wymondham, who was granted arms in 1664; W.Schenk, 1948, '*The Concern for Social Justice in the puritan Revolution*', p.177, n.4.

93. John Jubbes, May 4th 1649, '*An Apology Unto The honourable and worthy Officers*', p.2, T.T. E.552(28).

94. R.W.Ketton-Cremer, 1969, '*Norfolk in the Civil War*'.

95. PRO, SP 28/257 unfol., "*The Humble Peticion of Leftenant Colonell John Jubbes captain of a foot company under Sir Miles Hubbert his regiment and as Major under Coll Pickering, first under the command of the Lord Grey of Warke, and afterward upon his Reducement, in the army of the Right Honourable the earl of manchester from the year 1643 to the year 1645 as by the particulars full appears......*".

96. Holmes, op.cit.n.68, p.131.

97. Op.cit.n.95.

98. Bodleian Library, Ms Tanner 62 ff.426-7, quoted by Ketton-Cremer, op.cit.n.94, p.221.

99. Ketton-Cremer, op.cit.n.94, p.227 & 253.

100. Holmes, op.cit.n.68, p.176.

101. Wolfe, op.cit.n.18, p.3, referring to W.T.Whitley, 1923, '*A History of the British Baptists*', p.74-6.

102. Temple, op.cit.n.89, suggests this is Martin Husbands. He was in fact Azariah Husbands, '*Commons Journals*', vii, 39b; op.cit.n.68, p.176. He is possibly the Captain Husbands mentioned in Cromwell's letter of 1 Sept.1644 relating to the garrison at Lincoln, because the regiment was at Lincoln for a short time at the end of August 1644, Carlyle, op.cit.n.56, vol.1, p.155.

103. Sprigge, p.328.

104. Temple, op.cit.n.8, states that Captain Jenkins, who commanded the 3rd company in 1645, was George Jenkins, who died of his wounds at Drogheda. He says that the Captain Jenkins killed at Faringdon was a captain of horse. This cannot be right because Sprigge still records a Captain Jenkins in Cromwell's own regiment of horse in 1647. Moreover Sprigge states, p.328, that Captain Jenkins in Pickering's was John Jenkins who was killed at Faringdon in April 1645. That the same company came to be commanded by another Jenkins within two years of the death of its first Captain Jenkins is a coincidence, but it does not prove that Sprigge is in error. '*Commons Journals*', vii, 38b.

105. Sprigge, p.328; '*The True Informer*', 16th June 1645; Appendix 2 above.

106. A Major Cromwell in Colonel Ingoldsby's regiment was killed at the siege of Bristol in 1645. Sprigge, p.329.

107. Accounts, PRO, SP28/267, part 2, ff. 124-34.

108. Temple, op.cit.n.89; '*Commons Journals*', vii, 39b.

109. Temple, op.cit.n.89, suggests this was Thomas Price, who was Captain Lieutenant to Colonel Hewson in 1648, "*a gallant honest man*" who was killed at the battle of Maidstone. This seems unlikely as this would represent a demotion from captaincy.

110. Holmes, op.cit.68, p.162. George Williamson, '*Old Cartsburn*'. An engraving of Crawford was sold at Christies in 1984 (4/12/84 lot 175).

111. Harris, op.cit.n.57.

112. Op.cit.n.61.

113. Harris, op.cit.n.57, p.31, quoting an unnamed source.

114. Provost Marshall: responsible for discipline in the regiment, for the guarding of prisoners, and the regulating of the suttlers, R.Elton, 1650, *'The Compleat Body of the Art Military'*, p.180.

115. Quartermaster: responsible for arranging the quarters for the regiment; when at a siege organising the foraging for provisions; also skilled in mathematics to give directions for the fortifying and measuring of ground, Elton, op.cit.n.114, p.180.

116. Sergeant: to supervise the handling of arms; assist in the organisation of his division in marching and drilling, Elton, op.cit.n.114, p.181.

117. Gentleman at Arms: responsible for the maintenance and arranging of repair of arms and keeping records of the arms. Keeping the powder, bullet and match, Elton, op.cit.n.114, p.178.

118. Clerk of the Company: his chief duty to keep the Muster roll, receive money and pay the soldiers and keep a bill of payments and receipts, Elton, op.cit.n.114, p.177-8.

119. Corporal: took care of a squadron, instructing them in the use of their arms, and distributing food, powder, bullets and match to them, Elton, op.cit.n.114, p.179.

120. Gentleman of the Company: a soldier able enough to be a file leader, well skilled in the postures of arms, acting as a sentinel and accompanying the Captain of the Watch, Elton, op.cit.n.114, p.177.

121. Drum-major: a skilful drummer instructing all other drummers in the regiment, Elton, op.cit.n.114, p.178, and was usually in the Colonel's company, J.B., 1661, *'Some Brief Instructions for the Exercising of the Cavalry'*.

122. PRO, SP28/26 pt.I, f.293, f.308.

123. PRO, SP28/25 f.36, Axtell's account 18 April - 14 May, moneys lent to sick men at Hisson.

124. Unless otherwise stated, the sources used for the siege are J.Vicars, 1646, *'England's Parliamentary Chronicle'*, part 3, p.217-19, and contemporary accounts quoted by J.W.F.Hill, 1956, *'Tudor and Stuart Lincoln'*, p.157-8.

125. Vicars, op.cit.n.124.

126. Op.cit.n.30.

127. Bodleian Library, Carte Ms.74, f.159, Journal of Colonel Montague.

128. P.Wenham, 1970, *'The Great and Close Siege of York'*; Harris, op.cit.n.57.

129. *"We will go over the siege of York..."*, op.cit.n.30.

130. RCHM, 1972, *'The City of York : The Defences'*, p.24-6.

131. Col.H.C.B.Rogers, 1968, *'Battles and Generals of the Civil Wars'*.

132. Ashe's account of the battle in Vicars, op.cit.n.124, vol.3, p.269-282.

133. P.Newman, 1981, *'The Battle of Marston Moor 1644'*, p.112-114. D.Smurthwaite, 1993, *'The Complete Guide to the Battlefields of Britain'*, p.157-161.

134. *'Parliament Scout'* : 4-11 July 1644 ; T.T. E54 no.20.

135. *'A true relation of the late fight...'*, 8 July 1644, p.7, T.T.E54 no.7.

136. Wenham, op.cit.n.128, p.100.

137. S.R.Gardiner, 1893, *'History of the Great Civil War'*, vol.ii, p.20.

138. Petition of George Hancock, quoted by Wenham, op.cit. n.128, p.63.

139. Vicars, op.cit.n.124, part 4, p.7-21, claims Pickering was in command with Crawford and that there were 1200 foot. Various details in the following discussion of the brigade's actions are taken from *'A journal and a true and exact relation....under Maj.General Crayford'*, T.T. E.4(9).

140. P.Gaunt, 1987, *'Cromwellian Gazetteer'*, p.149; J. Holland, 1824, *'The Picture of Sheffield'*.

141. Montague op.cit.n.127. Vicars, op.cit.n.124, p.20. A.Polkey, 1992, *'The Civil War in the Trent Valley'*, p.46-7.

142. P.A.Faulkner, 1972, *'Bolsover Castle, Derbyshire: Official Handbook'*, p.16-18.

143. M.W.Thompson, 1987, *'The decline of the Castle'*. B.Stone, 1992, *'Derbyshire in the Civil War'*, p.63-65. Polkey, op.cit.n.141, p.47-9.

144. Op.cit.n.127; *'Journal...'*, op.cit.n.139; Vicars, op.cit.n.124, part 4, p.7-8.

145. *'Cal. of State Papers Domestic 1644'*, p.152-3. Clarendon, 1707, *'The History of the Rebellion and Civil Wars in England'*, II, p.418.

146. P.Harrington, 1992, *'Archaeology of the English Civil War'*, p.15-16, fig.2 & plates 4 & 5.

147. Clarendon, op.cit.n.145, chapter 16.

148. Godwin, op.cit.n.73, p.267.

149. J.Adair, (Ed.), 1981, *'They Saw It Happen: Contemporary Accounts of the Siege of Basing House'*, p.54.

150. Clarendon, op.cit.n.145, II, p.419; Montague's Journal, op.cit.n.127.

151. Godwin, op.cit.n.73, p.271-2.

152. Clarendon, op.cit.n.145, II, p.421.

153. J.Kinross, 1979, *'The Battlefields of Britain'*, p.80-1; Smurthwaite, op.cit.n.133; *'Cal.of State Papers Domestic 1644'*, p.150.

154. PRO, SP28/26 f.59, Captain Axtell's ensign lent money to his men at Newbury.

155. Harris, op.cit.n.57, p.49-51.

156. Clarendon, op.cit.n.145, VIII, p.422.

157. N.Pevsner, *'The Buildings of England: Berkshire'*, p.213; Gaunt, op.cit.n.140.

158. Clarendon, op.cit.n.145, p.421-3.

159. Gardiner, op.cit.n.137, p.54-61; Montague's Journal, op.cit.n.127.

160. Kingston, op.cit.n.49, p.170.

161. Davies, op.cit.n.65.

162. Holmes, op.cit.n.68, p.168.

163. Carver's company, *"three men paid 8 shillings a man and not allowed in the Muster coming up since"*, PRO, SP28/25 f.77.

164. Holmes, op.cit.n.68, p.238.

165. PRO, SP28/25, p.1.

166. PRO, SP28/25, f.34; SP28/25, f.195.

167. Holmes, op.cit.n.68, p.168.

168. PRO, SP28/267 f.93, 24th Feb 1645, £10/14/10 paid *"35 sick and wounded souldiers in the North that was left behind"*.

169. Wenham, op.cit.n.128, p.63.

170. PRO, SP28/25 f.60. PRO, SP28/128 f.126, Captain Husbands, 4th November, *"quarter of 3 soldiers being sick"*; f.138, Captain Gale, 4th November, 11 soldiers sick carry home; SP28/128 f.120, Hewson's company, 4th November, payment *"to 6 soldiers of yours 4/8d to carry them into their Countreys being sick"*; f.128, Captain Karver, 4th November, payment to 6 soldiers being sick to carry them home; f.136, Captain Silverwood, 4th November, payment for soldiers sick and sent home; f.138 Capt. Lieutenant Gale, Nov 4, 11 solders 4/8d a peece being sick to carry them home; f. 124, Capt. Axtell, 4 Nov, 8 solders of yours being sick ... to carry them home 4/8d a piece; f.126, Capt. Ware, payment to 7 soldiers to carry home being sick; f.136, Capt. Carter, Nov 4th, 3 soldiers sick to carry home.

171. PRO, SP28/24 f.520, *"Edward Webb Chirurgion his bill for cureing of maimed soldiers as followeth ..... Item for cureing one of Collonell Pickeringe soldier of a plurasie 5/- Item for cureing one other soldier of the said Collonells who was burned with gunpowder on the hand 5/-"*.

172. Eg: PRO, SP28/25, f.38, 22 men dead or run away; July, Jenkins', 21 men since dead or run away.

173. Vicars, op.cit.n.124, p.101; for the actions of his forces around Abingdon between December 1644 and April 1645, see Vicars part 4, p.93-5, 108, 126, 131-2.

174. PRO, SP28/25 f.202, pre 15 Dec. 1644, Lt. Gwyne under Captain Silverwood for conducting of soldiers from Sonning to Abingdon.

175. Davies, op.cit.n.65.

176. Rushworth, v, 804; Letter from Major General Browne, Commons Letter Books, January 11th repeated in T.T. E24(20). Gardiner, op.cit.n.137, vol.2, p.113.

177. Christopher Goodwine and Richard Thurston. Tibbutt, op.cit.n.54, no. 488.

178. T.Allen *'Abingdon: Vineyard Development'*, interim reports in *South Midlands Archaeology*, 1989, vol.19, p.44-6; 1990, vol.20, p.77-8; 1991, vol.21, p.98.

179. *'Cal. of State Papers Domestic 1644'*, p.151-2.

180. Carlyle, op.cit.n.56, p.149-50.

181. Godwin, op.cit.n.73, p.266.

182. Ketton-Cremer, op.cit.n.94, p.205.

183. Tibbutt, op.cit.n.54.

184. Temple, op.cit.n.102.

185. Carlyle, op.cit.n.56, p.149. Williamson, op.cit.n.110.

186. Vicars, op.cit.n.124, vol.4, p.98.

187. Temple, op.cit.n.89.

188. Silus Titus of Bushey, Essex, served under Ayloffe, VCH, *'Essex'*, Vol.2, p.33.

189. PRO, SP28/35 f.633, Letter from Hewson.

190. PRO, SP28/35 f.633, undated but presumably April 1645.

191. Godwin, op.cit.n.73, p.312.

192. Davies, op.cit.n.65, p.88-96.

193. Temple, op.cit.n.89.

194. *'Lords Journals'*, vii, ff.266 & 278; *'Commons Journals'*, iv, ff.26 & 64.

195. PRO, SP28/14 f.398, undated list of company commanders in Ayloffe's regiment in 1644: Col. Ayloffe, Major Badbury, Captains Whetston, Drumer, Titus, Robotham. The document also lists exact numbers of soldiers, drummers etc in each company but without names.

196. Gardiner, op.cit.n.137, vol.2, p.193.

197. PRO, SP28/267 f.95.

198. Davies, op.cit.n.65.

199. Eg: PRO, SP28/25 f.309, five weeks pay to Captain Carter because their pay behind the rest of the army, 14 Feb. 1645.

200. M.A.Kishlansky, *'The Rise of the New Model Army'*, p.67-8.

201. Whitacre's Diary, BL, Add.Ms. 31,116 fol.207 ; D'Ewes Diary: BL, Harl. Mss 166, fol.204b; quoted by Gardiner, op.cit.n.137, vol.2, p.193.

202. Tibbutt, op.cit.n.54, 1351, 9 June 1645.

203. *'An Order of Parliament "that no person be permitted to preach who is not ordained a Minister"'*. T.T.669.f.9(30).

204. Tibbutt, op.cit.n.54, 610.

205. Tibbutt, op.cit.n.54, 709, 9th(?) June 1645; Burditt was the commander of the Newport Pagnell garrison.

206. Sprigge, p.15.

207. S.Peachey and L.Prince, 1991, *'English Civil War Flags and Colours : English foot'*, p.46.

208. Carlyle, op.cit.n.56, vol.1, p.167-9.

209. Sprigge, p.328.

210. Sprigge, p.13.

211. Sprigge, 16; Clarendon, op.cit.n.145, IX, 28.

212. Gardiner, op.cit.n.137.

213. Tibbutt, op.cit.n.54, 1289.

214. PRO, SP28/140, part 2, f.6, bill paid by the General's order on 9th June 1645.

215. Tibbutt, op.cit.n.54, 709, ?9th June 1645.

216. Quoted by P.Young, 1985, *'Naseby, 1645'*, p.318.

217. Laing (Ed.), 1841, *'Baille's Letters and Journals'*, vol.1, p.286.

218. Holmes, op.cit.n.68, p.238.

219. Sprigge.

220. Op.cit.n.30.

221. *'The True Informer'*, 16th June 1645.

222. G.R.Foard, forthcoming, *'An Analysis of the Civil War Battlefield at Naseby'*, in *'Journal of Post Medieval Archaeology'*, 1995.

223. Sprigge, p.48-9. Vicars, op.cit.n.124, vol.4, p.171.

224. Sprigge, p.64-5; in the battle Fairfax had *"all his foot with him, save the Musketteers of 3 Regiments"*, Vicars, op.cit.n.124, vol.4, p.191; Carlyle, op.cit.n.56, 3, p.397-9.

225. Smurthwaite, op.cit.n.133; Sprigge.

226. Clarendon, op.cit.n.145, II, p.524.

227. Gaunt, op.cit.n.140, p.145.

228. Sprigge, p.69.

229. Vicars, op.cit.n.124, vol.4, p.198.

230. Sprigge, 66-74; Gardiner, op.cit.n.137, vol.2, p.273-4.

231. Sprigge, p.76.

232. Sprigge, p.77.

233. A.R.Bayley, 1910, *'The Great Civil War in Dorset'*, p.285. This provides a detailed account of the siege of Sherborne Castle.

234. Vicars, op.cit.n.124, vol.4, p.255.

235. *"Cavetain passe is to be kept by Col.Montague and Col.Pickering, they went thither the 20th at night...."*, *'Moderate Intelligencer'*, Thurs. 21 Aug. to Thurs 28th Aug.1645.

236. Sprigge, p.95.

237. Carlyle, op.cit.n.56, vol.1, p.183.

238. Anon, 1868, *'The sieges of Bristol during the Civil War'*.

239. Op.cit.n.30.

240. Carlyle, op.cit.n.56, p.245, letter dated 14 Sept.1645; Sprigge, p.114.

241. Carlyle, op.cit.n.56, p.247; Sprigge, p.117.

242. Sprigge, p.106.

243. *'A true relation of the storming of Bristol...'*, 11th Sept. 1645, T.T. E301 no.5.

244. Young, op.cit.n.6, p.293.

245. Sprigge, p.128.

246. Clarendon, op.cit.n.145, vol.2, p.545.

247. Sprigge, p.122.

248. Anon, 1859, '*A History Military and Municipal of the Ancient Borough of the Devizes*', p.243. This makes an unreferenced statement that Pickering received a reply from the governor of Laicock on 23rd September. This was the day that Devizes surrendered, implying that Pickering's were not at Devizes throughout the whole siege.

249. VCH, 1975, '*Wiltshire*', vol.X, p.232; Gaunt, op.cit.n.140.

250. Sprigge, p.124-5.

251. J.Burnett-Brown, 1988, '*Lacock Abbey, Wiltshire*'.

252. '*Perfect Passages*', 1 Oct.1645 P.Young & W.Emberton, 1978, '*Sieges of the Great Civil War*', p.82-87; A detailed account of the siege of Winchester is given by Godwin, op.cit.n.73, p.332-343.

253. Quoted by Godwin, op.cit.n.73, p.339.

254. '*City Scout*', 11 Oct. 1645.

255. '*True Informer*', 4th Oct. 1645; '*Exact Journal*', 7th October 1645.

256. Carlyle, op.cit.n.56, p.251, letter from Cromwell, 28th September 1645; Sprigge, p.128.

257. Carlyle, op.cit.n.56, vol.1, p.189.

258. Godwin, op.cit.n.73, p.341.

259. '*A Description of the Siege of Basing Castle kept by the Lord Marquis of Winchester, 1645*', quoted by Adair, op.cit.n.73. Young & Emberton, op.cit.n.88-98; W.Emberton, 1972, '*Love Loyalty - the Close and Perilous Siege of Basing House 1643-45*'.

260. VCH, 1911, '*Hampshire*', vol.4, p.115 et seq.; S.Moorhouse, '*Finds from Basing House, Hampshire*', in '*Post Medieval Archaeology*'.

261. '*Scottish Dove*', Friday 17th Oct. 1645, quoted by Godwin, op.cit.n.73, p.349.

262. '*Mercurius Civicus*', 22nd October 1645.

263. Carlyle, op.cit.n.56, p.254, letter, 14th October 1645.

264. Adair, op.cit.n.73, p.76.

265. '*Weekly Account*', TT E.305,19; '*The True Informer*', 9th October 1645; '*Cal. of State Papers Domestic 1645-1647*', p.190.

266. Godwin, op.cit.n.73, p.270.

267. Carlyle, op.cit.n.56, vol.1, p.197.; '*Mercurius Civicus*', 8th October; '*Moderate Intelligencer*', 7th October.

268. Gaunt, op.cit.n.140, p.172.

269. Sprigge, p.146; Bayley, op.cit.n.133, p.296-7.

270. Whitelock, '*Memorials*', p.190, quoted by J.Hutchins, 1861, '*History and Antiquities of the County of Dorset*', vol.1, p.508.

271. Sprigge, p.207, news received by Fairfax on 6th March.

272. Sprigge, p.154.

273. Quoted by Godwin, op.cit.n.73, p.341.

274. Sprigge, p.155.

275. W.C.Abbott (Ed.), 1937, '*The Writings and Speeches of Oliver Cromwell*', p.391; J.Whitam, 1984, '*Ottery St.Mary*', p.44-5.

276. Polwhele, 1826, '*Traditions and Recollections*'; the letter is reprinted from Polwhele, with errors, in Carlyle, op.cit.n.56, vol.3, p.395-6. The reference by Carlyle to Pendennis Castle follows Polwhele's misreading of the original document, now in the Bodleian Library, '*Select Clarendon Papers*', vol.ix, I. The corrected version is given in Abbott, op.cit.n.275, p.391.

277. Sprigge, p.128. Ceely was still governor in October 1645.

278. Devon Record Office, Burial Registers for Ottery St.Mary.

279. Dryden's first published work, in 1659, was to be a eulogy, '*A Poem upon the death of his late Highness, Oliver, Lord Protector of England, Scotland and Ireland*'.

280. Bethel was a Major killed in the siege of Bristol, Sprigge, p.142.

281. Op.cit.n.30.

282. '*The Kingdom's Scout*', 2nd-9th December 1645.

283. This and the following notes are marginal in Sprigge's text. "*Proffered ransomes*"

284. "*He had done the Kingdome great service, by riding between England and Scotland before these troubles.*"

285. "*The Army rested then some time at Autree*"

286. "*The Army was unworthily censured at that time, as is observed before in the Story*".

287. "*He was a little man, but of great courage*"

288. "*the Heavens*"

289. Sprigge, p.156. A prose poem to Pickering is said to exist in John Cooke, 1646, '*Vindication of the Law*', but I have been unable to trace a copy of this book.

290. Hewson was still recorded as Lt.Colonel as late as June 1646. Sprigge, p.277, list of officers at the Council of War at the Oxford siege.

291. 13th May 1647, Clarke MSS, vol.41, f.119.

292. Wolfe, op.cit.n.18, p.142-153.

293. Wolfe, op.cit.n.92, p.311-2.

294. Temple, op.cit.n.102; the statement made at the Army Council of 1 Nov.1647, the Putney Debate, A.S.P.Woodhouse, '*puritanism and Liberty*', p.99-100; Gardiner, op.cit.n.196, vol.3, p.234; John Jubbes, 1648, '*Several Proposals for Peace and Freedom*', reprinted in Wolfe, op.cit.n.18.; W.Schenk, 1948, '*The concern for social justice and the puritan revolution*'.

295. Schenk, op.cit.n.92, p.73. The first two political documents of the millenarian cause came out of Norwich, Jubbes' home town, and addressed the issues expressed elsewhere by Jubbes. B.S.Capp, 1972 '*The Fifth Monarchy Men*', p.52-5.

296. Wolfe, op.cit.n.92, p.97, 368, 377-8.

297. Quoted by A.Fraser, 1985, '*Cromwell our Chief of Men*', p.310.

298. C.Firth and G.Davies, 1940, '*The Regimental History of Cromwell's Army*', vol.2, p.406-7; Noble, op.cit.n.7, vol.1, p.328. Noble's statement that Husbands replaced Axtell as Major in 1648 is not correct for he had been replaced by Grimes as Captain of the 1st company by 1647. Azariah Husbands was by the close of 1646 a captain in Rich's regiment of horse, replacing Captain Dendy, rising to Major by 1647. He acquitted himself extremely well during the 1648 clearance of the castles of Kent; Noble, p.324; Sprigge p.328-30; Firth and Davies, p.144-9; Carter was major by summer 1648, Firth & Davies p.407; he was replaced c.1650 by Arnop who became Lt.Col. in about 1651; Thomas Price became Captain Lieutenant to Colonel Hewson in 1648, "*a gallant honest man*" killed at Maidstone, Temple, op.cit.89.

299. Fairfax Correspondence, vol.4, p.32-3.

300. Temple, op.cit.n.89; DNB.

301. G.A.Raikes, 1878, '*The History of the Honourable Artillery Company*'.

302. Firth and Davies, op.cit.n.298, p.158-160.

303. Firth & Davies, op.cit.n.298, p.417.

304. Bodleian Library, Carte Ms 74, f.159.

Index

146

PORTRAITS

OF THE

PARLIAMENTARY OFFICERS

OF THE

Great Civil War ;

The Religious succeſsfull and truly Valliant Lieutenant Generall Cromwell

The twenty portraits of Parliamentary Officers are faithfully reproduced from facsimiles of prints first published by Ricraft in 1647, now extremely rare. There is a short biography of each officer taken from a limited edition of this work (100 copies) published in 1873.

Size 21cm x 14.5cm
64 Pages Paperback
ISBN 0 946014 08 6   POST FREE **£4**.⁹⁵

A full list of our publications sent free on request. Pryor Publications, 75, Dargate Road, Yorkletts, Whitstable, Kent CT5 3AE 0227 274655.

If you would like information on Col. John Pickering's Regiment of the Sealed Knot please contact Glenn Foard 0604 811618 or Alan Pryor 0227 274655.